TROUBLE AT T'MILL

The 1826 Yorkshire Weavers' Riots

George Ingle

Illustrations by students from
Ilkley Grammar School

RP

Published by Royd Press
The Book Case
29 Market Street
Hebden Bridge
West Yorks.
HX7 6EU
www.bookcase.co.uk

Cover design: D&P Design and Print

ISBN: 978-1-907197-11-6

By the same author:

Yorkshire Cotton, Preston, 1997

Textile Manufacture in Keighley. (John Hodgson, Keighley 1879). Facsimile reprint, with an introduction and index by Gillian Cookson and George Ingle. Stamford, 1999

Marriner's Yarns, Lancaster, 2004

Yorkshire Dales Textile Mills, Hebden Bridge, 2009

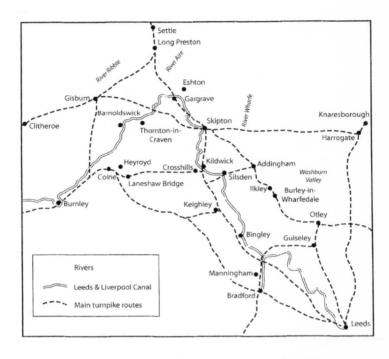

Routes taken by the rioters and military

Sources and Acknowledgements

I have taken inspiration from William Turner's book, *Riot*, which tells the story of the East Lancashire weavers' riots in 1826. Over a thousand power looms were smashed in dozens of mills, compared with only twenty-five destroyed in one mill in Yorkshire. However, though the damage caused by the rioting in Yorkshire was small, fear and panic was widespread. Destruction of the hated new machines was only avoided by Yorkshire mill owners using weapons and soldiers to defend their mills. The resolute and successful defence of two mills by the Horsfall brothers in Addingham and Bradford prevented the rioting spreading any further in the county. Thousands of people watched, or took part in the Yorkshire disturbances, but they were not repeated, so little has been written about the events and nothing remains in folk memory about the desperate efforts of the hand-loom weavers to redress their grievances and smash the new power looms.

The advent of the internet, and the growing digitisation of historical records, has made the task of the historical researcher so much easier. For earlier books on local textile history I had to visit libraries and archives in Leeds, London and elsewhere. Now the internet has provided access to back copies of local newspapers and also Home Office records which have provided the bulk of the material in this book. My thanks therefore go to the people and organisations who are working hard to make historical information available to anyone with a computer.

As this is not intended as a scholarly work, detailed references have been omitted. However, I have tried to indicate from where particular pieces of information have been derived. For instance, the issue of the *Leeds Mercury* for the relevant date mentioned in the text will usually provide the full report on the incident. The Home Office Correspondence file HO40/19 & 20, which again is available on-line from the Public Record Office, has copies of letters and documents relating to the disturbances in Yorkshire and elsewhere.

My research into Yorkshire textile history has again been encouraged by my good friend and noted textile historian Chris Aspin, who kindly read through and improved the original manuscript. The map was produced by Mike Clarke, who was able to add information about turnpike trusts to his extensive knowledge of canal history. John Hansen, from the Bradford Historical and Antiquarian Society, kindly provided a photograph of North Wing Mill in Bradford before its demolition. Dr Bob Ducket, the editor of their journal, *The Bradford Antiquary*, led me to articles written in 1881 and 1884 about the 1825 strike of wool combers and weavers and also these riots. Similarly Don Barrett from the Addingham Civic Society gave me the photograph of Low Mill in

Addingham at the height of its expansion to be the largest textile mill in the Yorkshire Dales.

I approached my old school, Ilkley Grammar School, to see if any students would be interested in providing illustrations based on the text. Gillian James, the Head, instantly agreed, and together with Head of Art, Louise Mortimer, asked for volunteers. Six students prepared drawings. Katherine Robinson, Lydia Watson, Sophie Parnaby, Charlotte Smith, Josephine Lingard, and Lillian Baldwin brought the story to life, and I am deeply grateful to them. I wish them well in their future careers.

Finally I would like to thank Felicity Potter and Kate Claughan from Royd Press for both taking on the publication of this book and their hard work in putting it together ready for printing. We all owe so much to small publishing firms, which support the growing interest in local history.

Contents

Illustrations

INTRODUCTION

For a few days in the spring of 1826, machine-breaking riots convulsed the Yorkshire textile districts, where power looms had begun to weave cloth. Soldiers defending a Bradford mill shot dead a young man trying to break in; another ball killed a boy of thirteen. Five men and a boy aged seven were wounded. The defenders of an Addingham mill repulsed the attackers after an exchange of fire with many wounded, but at Gargrave, a mob met no opposition and smashed twenty-five looms.

Widespread starvation, especially among hand-loom weavers, who believed the new machines were robbing them of their livelihood, prompted the disturbances, which brought a swift response from mill owners, magistrates and the military.

I live less than two miles from Low Mill, near Addingham in the Yorkshire Dales. Built in 1787, it was the first in Yorkshire to spin worsted yarn and textile processing finally finished there in 2004. Over the years I have written books and articles about many Yorkshire mills, but Low Mill always held a special interest. I knew the story of the starving weavers who attacked the building in 1826. I also knew that rioters had attacked a mill in Bradford some days later. What I wasn't aware of was the full reason for the riots, what exactly happened and the link between the two incidents.

About seventy years after they occurred, Harry Speight, in his book *Upper Wharfedale,* described the riots at Low Mill in Addingham, and William Cudworth's *Manningham, Heaton and Allerton* covered the riots at North Wing Mill in Bradford. The surprising coincidence was that the men who ran the two mills were brothers, Jeremiah Horsfall at Addingham and John Horsfall at Bradford. Their father had been a partner at a Clitheroe mill in Lancashire which was nearly attacked at the same time and which was run by their cousin Jeremiah Garnett from Otley. William Turner in his book *Riot* gave a comprehensive account of the Lancashire riots, but did not connect the owners of Low Moor Mill, near Clitheroe, or the events there, with the attacks on the two mills run by the Horsfall brothers in Yorkshire.

The reason for the alarm in the area was the fear of rioting and attacks on mills by hand-loom weavers and others, perhaps from Lancashire, though most of the people involved in the Yorkshire riots were local. For four days, from Monday 24th until Thursday the 27th of April, 1826, starving hand-loom weavers in central and east Lancashire attacked textile mills in that area to smash the new power looms which they believed were destroying their livelihoods. The determined men and women operated in large crowds, in the open, and during the day. They were not all unemployed weavers, but included many others who lived in the same villages and saw the local economy collapsing. The outbreaks of violence seemed to start spontaneously, initially without leaders and spread by imitation. The rioters were normally law-abiding people, but were sufficiently incensed by the apparent lack of concern about their condition to take the law into their own hands. They had a strong sense of community, but no collective voice and no immediate restraints when they realised that their way of life was being destroyed. It has since been described as 'collective bargaining' by riot. On the Wednesday and Thursday of the same week, and the Monday and Wednesday of the following week, the rioting spread to Yorkshire.

In putting together this account I have mainly used local newspapers, which were published weekly. The papers at the time had six columns of dense text and largely copied material from each other, particularly the more local papers. News of events from around the world featured and what we now see as major events were lost among items which today we would think as having little interest. The local papers depended on reports being sent to the editor by anyone who was at the scene and the

A Gentleman

reports could contain a great deal of exaggerated rumour and speculation about the extent of the unrest. As few ordinary people were literate the reports generally reflected the views of 'gentlemen' who supported the authorities. However, there was at least one letter from someone who understood the changes taking place in the local textile industry and after the events provided a reason for the disturbances.

One important eye-witness account came from the editor of the *Bradford & Huddersfield Courier*, Henry Inglis, who left his office and followed the mob through Bradford on the afternoon of Wednesday 3rd May 1826. When they all arrived at North Wing Mill, he stood on a wall to have a better view of the proceedings for his report later that week. However, when the gunfire started he wisely ducked down behind the wall he had been standing on, but he was still able to report on what he saw and heard. In the absence of any more detailed accounts of the movements of the rioters, and their actions at the three Yorkshire mills, the newspaper reports have provided most of the information. However, the eyewitness stories have been substantiated by a coroner's report and the newspaper accounts of later court proceedings. Several men were arrested and examined by the magistrates and some of them were sent with an armed escort for trial at the Summer Assizes at York. Some were sentenced to death.

Further information has come from a selection of Home Office papers. These are letters which were sent by local magistrates and clergymen to the Home Office as well as reports from the military commanders in the region. Most were addressed to Sir Robert Peel who was Secretary of State for what was then called the Home Department, but some were sent to Henry Hobhouse who was the permanent under-secretary of state for the Home Department. I have used the term 'Home Secretary' for convenience.

BACKGROUND

At the end of the eighteenth century mill villages were thriving in Airedale and Wharfedale. It must be remembered that the assumption that the cotton and worsted industries were based respectively in Lancashire and Yorkshire, with no overlap, was not true at this time. Low Mill in Addingham was on an excellent water-powered site and was able to take the full flow of the river. By 1820 there were three other mills in the village, spinning cotton and worsted. Three further mills were added later in the nineteenth century. Burley-in-Wharfedale had the large cotton-spinning mill known as Greenholme Mill, also on the river Wharfe. This was built in 1792 and changed hands in 1810. The new owners, Greenwood & Ellis from Keighley, built a large new mill, installed gas lighting, but kept Jonas Whitaker, a former partner, as managing partner. They installed 108 power looms in 1825. Three other mills were built at Burley-Wood-Head fed by a reservoir on the moor. Otley had cotton-spinning mills from 1787, as did most villages further up Wharfedale from Addingham. These included Hartlington, Linton, Grassington, Kettlewell, Arncliffe and others. Much of the cotton yarn produced at these mills was woven locally by hundreds of hand-loom weavers, but power looms were being installed in increasing numbers in Lancashire, and by 1826, in some Yorkshire mills. It is important to remember that many of these early mills were built for spinning cotton yarn and that the commercial centre for that industry was Manchester.

In Airedale, Gargrave had three cotton-spinning mills by 1800 while Skipton and Bingley had several, both in the towns and in the surrounding valleys. The first combined worsted and cotton mill in Bradford wasn't built until 1800, but easy access to coal supplies and the development of steam power meant that the town was on the way to becoming 'Worstedopolis' by the end of the century. By 1820 Bradford had outstripped the older worsted producing areas in England and the first experiments with power-loom weaving took place there in 1822. The weaving of cotton by power looms was already well established in parts of Lancashire and the looms were then adapted to weave worsted cloth. The first worsted looms for a Bradford mill were destroyed before they could be installed, but in 1824 the firm of J G Horsfall designed, built and set to work worsted power looms at their mill at North Wing, Bradford. However, the introduction of power looms elsewhere to weave worsted was slow for a number of reasons and surprisingly, worsted power looms were not introduced into the mills in Keighley until the mid-1830s.

THE FAMILIES AND THEIR MILLS

This account identifies the links between some of the textile families who were victims of the rioting, how they reacted to the threats, and the general background to the riots. The mechanisation of cotton spinning in the new mills in Yorkshire from 1780 had swept away the old hand-spinning wheels and provided abundant yarn for thousands of hand-loom weavers in Yorkshire and across the border in Lancashire. The same machines were then adapted to spin worsted yarn from 1787. This in turn boosted supplies to the domestic worsted weavers and their hand looms, who supplied the ever-increasing national and international demand for cloth. Inevitably, however, technology moved on and there was pressure to mechanise the next stage in the production of cloth after spinning. The early problems of how to weave cotton yarn on a power loom had been overcome. About forty years after the building of cotton-, and later worsted-spinning mills in Yorkshire, and the consequent huge increase in the supply of yarn, power looms became readily available and mill owners started to install them in their mills. However, they soon realised that the looms, because of their vibration, needed a firm foundation. As a result single-storey weaving sheds were later built alongside the multi-storey spinning mills.

Two generations of the Horsfall and Garnett families demonstrate the growth of the textile industries in the area during the first part of the century. Timothy Horsfall was born in 1764 and began his working life as a tanner before renting Goit Stock Mill near Bingley, in 1791. Horsfall's partners in this cotton-spinning venture were James Anderton, his brother-in-law, who was also described as a 'gentleman', and Richard Holdsworth, a maltster from Otley who was also a partner at Low Mill at West End in the Washburn Valley. By 1797 Anderton had left the partnership, but Thomas Colbeck from Keighley and John Horsfall from Bradford had joined the firm at Goit Stock.

Timothy Horsfall married Sarah Garnett in 1785. She was the sister of Jeremiah Garnett from Otley, who ran the paper mill on the river Wharfe, making press papers. Timothy and Sarah Horsfall had several children and with their combined wealth were able to expand the textile interests of both families, the Horsfalls and the Garnetts.

In 1799 Timothy, and his brother-in-law, Jeremiah Garnett, took Low Moor Mill near Clitheroe for cotton spinning. The firm traded as Garnett & Horsfall with Jeremiah's second son, also Jeremiah, as managing partner. By 1824 the mill had more than a hundred power looms weaving 2,500 pieces a week. The Lancashire rioters twice advanced on the mill, but it was too well defended for them to cause damage. In later years the firm was very successful, importing cotton from their own plantations in Virginia on their own ships. The mill was later enlarged and weaving sheds added.

Advertisement from Leeds Mercury, 11th May 1822

Timothy Horsfall died in 1811, but his young sons took over the running of Goit Stock Mill. By the 1820s the six brothers wished to expand, following the example of their uncle and cousin. Low Mill at Addingham had recently become available to rent or for sale. The mill was owned by Ellis Cunliffe then living at Manningham House, near Bradford, and had been used for worsted spinning by Pullan & Co, but was advertised to let or for sale in 1820 and 1822. This was then a substantial mill with two water wheels and was said to be capable of running five to six thousand spindles. There was also a warehouse and twenty-four cottages. Jeremiah Horsfall took the property in 1824 on a twenty-year lease and started cotton spinning, soon adding power looms. He then added a larger mill, end on to the original building. As Farfield Hall, on the road to Bolton Abbey, was vacant on the death of William Cunliffe, Ellis Lister's brother, it was also taken by Jeremiah Horsfall. Ellis Cunliffe had changed his name to Cunliffe-Lister when he married into the Bradford Lister family, and later to Ellis Cunliffe-Lister-Kay.

Jeremiah's younger brother, John Garnett Horsfall, together with William, Michael, Timothy and Thomas took North Wing Mill in Bradford in 1823. Thomas acted as mill manager while William bought the raw wool. John James, writing in 1857, explained that John Horsfall *"... having a bent of mind towards mechanical pursuits, devoted much time, with the aid of an ingenious mechanist, to surmount the difficulties which obstructed the successful manufacture of worsted by these (power) looms, and in consequence several of them were set up in the mill ..."*

The company traded as John Garnett Horsfall & Co. and installed these power looms in 1824. This was a large five-storey steam powered mill used for both spinning and weaving worsted, not cotton. Out of all the mills visited by the rioters in Lancashire and Yorkshire, only these three mills, run by the Horsfall/Garnett families were so well defended that no looms were destroyed.

North Wing Mill, Bradford before demolition

The Horsfall brothers were relatively affluent. Timothy lived at Hawkesworth Hall, Thomas at Burley Hall and William at Calverley Hall.

The other Yorkshire mill visited by the rioters was in Gargrave. None of the reports says precisely which mill was attacked and the evidence is confusing. There were three textile mills in Gargrave and one report suggests that it was the mill at Middle Green, Goffa or Low Mill, which was attacked. I originally thought that it was Airebank Mill, but more detailed research indicates that it was High Mill. This three-storey mill, which is still standing, is on the site of a corn mill and was built by Joseph Mason. He was sixty-eight at the time and perhaps wanted to provide a future for a nephew with the same name. Another nephew,

Thomas Mason ran Airebank Mill, hence the confusion. Joseph Mason junior was listed as a cotton manufacturer at High Mill in 1822 and would have been having his yarn woven locally by hand-loom weavers. His uncle died in 1823 and by 1826 Joseph had invested in twenty-five power looms to replace the work of some of the weavers around the village and further afield. The cloth woven by the local weavers, and now on his new power looms, was sent to Manchester for dyeing and finishing.

LIFE IN THE 1820s

It is difficult to see the disturbances of the time from a modern perspective. The events of nearly 200 years ago are puzzling to understand unless we take into account the huge changes which have taken place in how we live. It is hard to imagine the lives of the poorest hand-loom weavers living in the most basic conditions with little food and large families to feed. The period after the end of the Napoleonic wars in 1815 was a time of great instability in trade, particularly the textile trades. There had been good years with high wages, but by 1826 life was extremely hard for thousands of local people. The basic diet was oatmeal taken with water, which in bad times was the only food available. If there was no work at all, the option was the workhouse which separated families and from which, with no money, there was no escape. The unemployed could also ask for outdoor relief from their parish. This was a small amount of money to buy food, usually oats, paid for by the owners of land or property in the parish. The state resisted providing any help as Parliament decided that any state help would stop the flow of charitable aid for the destitute. If people were poor and starving that was judged to be their problem, though charity was widely encouraged and help did come from many parts of the country.

When demand for cloth was low, the weavers were at the mercy of the manufacturers who 'put out' the yarn. The cost of a loom was small and the 'putting-out' system where weavers worked for a manufacturer was widespread. The weaver took yarn from the manufacturer and returned a piece of cloth. If he was industrious and careful he could set up as a manufacturer himself and employ others. Some manufacturers dealt with a dozen or so weavers, others with hundreds, while some had

Handloom weaver at work

a putting-out room at their spinning mill and combined spinning with weaving. However, trade was volatile and even in good times the relative prosperity of the hand-loom weavers was subject to trade depressions and a gradual erosion of standards. Periods of high wages brought in people with no training and apprenticeships lapsed. Poor trade, particularly when peace came in 1815, brought ruthless competition with a gradual reduction in wages. Prices were cut and weavers had to work longer for less pay. All attempts by the weavers to organise and petition for help or appeal to the authorities were seen as potentially revolutionary and therefore repressed.

In 1816, William Sidgwick, a cotton spinner at High Mill in Skipton, told a Parliamentary inquiry that he sold most of his yarn to manufacturers in his own neighbourhood. There were many weavers in the area who were working long hours.

The independence of many weavers was gradually eroded as larger manufacturers set up weaving shops. Addingham had two and there were several in Skipton, including one run by William Chamberlain from Eastby Mill. These loom shops were a half-way-house between the domestic weaver determining his own work rate, however long, and the new water- or steam-powered weaving sheds working regular hours. What they did stop was the embezzlement of yarn by the weavers working in their own homes. As wages were lowered by competition among the weavers themselves, distress and starvation became widespread, with seemingly no solution, or any attempt to find one, by the government. Though the new power looms were blamed for the lack of work for the hand-loom weavers it was the periodic depressions in trade for all occupations which were the root of the problem.

The early establishment of cotton-spinning mills in West Yorkshire from 1780 had created a successful industry, which continued until the twentieth century. Skipton and the surrounding mill villages, including Addingham, had cotton mills until the 1950s and there was no sharp frontier between cotton and worsted.

The weavers and others involved in the two separate riots lived and worked in the same conditions. It just so happened that the recent introduction of worsted power looms in Bradford coincided with the extensive riots in the cotton areas and led to a reason for the riots there.

Again, many textile processes which today are carried out in factories or mills were done by hand in the home or workshops. Thousands of men, women and children still worked in that way in West Yorkshire. That was particularly true in the small towns and villages where most people lived before the expansion of the industrial towns. Hand spinning was no longer viable, but hand knitting was widespread, particularly in the Northern Dales and there is still a Stockinger Lane in Addingham. Hand-loom weaving and hand combing were the most common occupations in the region. The frequently quoted comment of Napoleon Bonaparte that the English were a nation of shopkeepers referred to workshops, not retail shops.

There had been an earlier attempt to introduce power looms in the Bradford area in 1822. A worsted manufacturer named Warwick had a loom made to weave worsted cloth. It was most certainly adapted from a cotton loom and was installed secretly in a mill in Shipley. When its arrival became known, hand-loom weavers from the area surrounded the mill and demanded that it be removed. As the loom was being taken away on a cart protected by special constables, the weavers overcame the constables, smashed the loom and dragged the roller, with the warp threads still on it, up to the village of Baildon where many weavers lived.

The development of the power loom advanced in stages similar to that of other complicated machines. Though the Rev. Edmund Cartwright patented the first power loom in 1785 it was not until the early 1820s that the machine became established. By 1826, a year of acute distress, there were enough looms to turn the hand-loom weavers' fear of them to outright hostility. The three Yorkshire mills attacked by the rioters were run by men who had previously put out their yarn to be woven, and who replaced some of this work with power looms.

It is difficult to understand the attitude of the various groups involved in the rioting if we apply modern thinking. Social, political and economic ideas were so different at the time when, for example, the French Revolution, which swept away the king and the aristocracy in France, was still fresh in the minds of those in authority. By and large social unrest was dealt with harshly as it was seen as a possible precursor to overthrowing the government, though that was far from the minds of the local weavers. Those in authority felt that suppression of all attempts by weavers and others to gain a decent wage and freedom from poverty was necessary for the continuation of the state as it was.

Economic theory was based on an acceptance of trade cycles and the feeling that government should not interfere with 'trade'.

Individuals were seen as responsible for their own salvation. There were no obvious barriers to a few people rising out of humble beginnings to become reasonably well to do and employing others. Each town in the textile areas had examples of these people. However, they were rare and the vast majority of workers suffered when demand for their labour declined. These workers on the other hand could not understand why those in authority did nothing about their suffering. Many thought that the king and his government did not help them because they were unaware of their situation. Petitions and marches were organised to get the message to them, but these were ignored or broken up as being provocative. The public meeting held on the 16th August, 1819 in St. Peter's Field, Manchester to consider means of reforming or repealing the Corn Laws was broken up by the yeoman cavalry and eight people were killed. Peterloo reminded people of the way magistrates could use local militia units against them.

Two other opposing attitudes were also common and, understandably, remain today. The first was the worry of anyone in a job who soon could be made redundant by the introduction of machinery. This was an essential element of the industrial revolution, which, it can be argued, continues today with the replacement of human labour or intelligence by machine. Those who suffered with the introduction of power looms vented their anger on the looms as they could see no alternative. Those that could afford to stand back from the dispute looked at a wider picture. The counter-argument was that mechanisation and industrialisation until then had resulted in vastly increased production, wealth and the creation of more jobs. The other argument was that the workers, who didn't understand that their problems were temporary, needed to be educated into the reality of progress. If only they would be patient, things would get better and anyway, nothing could stop the introduction of new machinery. This was not a message to which the starving weavers were prepared to listen.

It can be argued that social class divisions are still relevant to us today. Even now there appears to be a widening gap between the poorest and richest sections of our population, which is thought to be very divisive. However, the gap in 1826 was well known and accepted. Phrases such as "the lower orders" were used and the concept of "rank" with "clergy and gentlemen" seen as superior, was well established. In addition, of course, there was no political voice for most people, as they did not have a vote. However, there appeared to be a strong sense of charitable responsibility among some of the wealthier sections of society when "working men" were unemployed and destitute. Women were rarely if ever mentioned. Workhouses existed, but quickly became full. For a family to enter a workhouse meant splitting the father from mother and children and as they had nothing, their chances of starting life again outside were slight. Parish relief of money or, more likely distribution of basic food stuffs such as oats, was the norm. It should be remembered that until the building of turnpike roads and canals, nearly all West Riding towns and villages had relied on locally-grown oats as their basic diet. Oats were ground at the local corn mill, which existed in every town and village and were made into large round flat oat-cakes or havercakes. In hard times the oats were eaten with hot water in a type of porridge and that was often the only food people had, every day of the week. Much of the 'relief' provided for the starving during this time was a measured quantity of oatmeal. The sites of these old mills, sometimes from medieval times, had provided ideal situations for the new textile mills in the Yorkshire Dales including High Mill in Gargrave.

Making oatcakes

Another important group of local people, the clergy, played a significant role during the riots. At the time the phrase 'clergy and gentlemen' was widely used. Clergymen of the

Church of England studied classics at Oxford or Cambridge and were often the younger sons of the landed gentry who therefore could not inherit any part of the family estate and went into the clergy instead of the army or colonial service. They had a variety of roles within the community as well as conducting the church services. They could be magistrates or attend meetings of the Poor Law guardians. If there was a school in the parish they would be involved as well as with local charities. Their own land-owning or other business interests would also take their time and some had private pupils. The actions of two local clergymen show the diversity that was possible. The Rev. Lamplugh Hird was a prebendary of York and vicar of Paull in Holderness, East Yorkshire, both of which gave him an income for minimum duties. However, his marriage into the Hird family at Low Moor Ironworks meant that he lived at Low Moor, dispensed justice as a magistrate at Low Moor Chapel House and managed his land and other business interests in the area. He was the local magistrate who read the Riot Act at the Bradford riots. In contrast, the Rev. Mordaunt Barnard, who was the permanent curate for the parishes of Thornton and Barnoldswick, raised money locally to relieve the poverty among the starving weavers in his area of Craven and when that proved insufficient sought extra money from the Home Secretary, pleading that his parishioners were 'starving in silence'. The Rev. Henry Heap, vicar of Bradford made a similar appeal.

Another element, which is foreign to us after nearly two hundred years, is the great change in the way any laws were maintained. The Lord Lieutenant of the county, with his deputy, was responsible for maintaining law and order in the county. This power was devolved to the magistrates or Justices of the Peace. In the days when most people knew each other, criminals were only traced when someone informed on them or they were caught in the act. The magistrate could bind them to keep the peace or could imprison them with the help of the parish constable, if there was one. Those committing serious offences were sent to York Castle to be tried at the assizes. Special constables, then as now, were ordinary members of the public, who were sworn in when there was an emergency. They could, at times, infiltrate the mob of rioters and gather evidence to be used later against offenders.

Two judges travelled round the country from the courts in Westminster to hear cases at the assizes several times a year. The penal code was very severe, with more than 200 capital offences, including rioting. The juries often asked for leniency and instead of the death penalty offenders were transported to Australia. In some cases a prison sentence was substituted.

In times of serious trouble, a magistrate could call upon the regular army or the yeomanry, but remained in charge. In 1824 the country's yeomanry regiments had been placed into districts to increase efficiency. The West Riding Yeomanry was linked with the

Lancashire units in one division with the Craven regiment based at Skipton. This Yeoman Cavalry regiment was commanded by Lord Ribblesdale. In addition, at times of a serious disturbance, the magistrate could read a passage from the Riot Act to any group of more than twelve people, which meant that they had to disperse within an hour. The Riot Act had been introduced in 1714 and was not repealed until 1967. If the crowd did not disperse, the special constables, or the militia involved, were indemnified against killing or injuring the people involved. This meant that live ammunition could be used by military units against people who had not dispersed and were rioting. The act also made it a felony, punishable by death, if people in a riot caused, or began to cause, serious damage to places of worship, houses, barns and stables. Mills and machines were not mentioned, but judges took them to be included. If buildings were damaged the residents of the local authority, the hundred, were liable to pay damages to the owners. This law was used to compensate mill owners in Lancashire and Yorkshire whose power looms were smashed.

An officer

Armed resistance to rioting was allowed in certain circumstances even though the Riot Act had not been read.

The authorities deployed armed forces in what was called the 'northern manufacturing district', which meant that troops could be moved round at short notice to places where disturbances existed or were expected to break out. Small parties of men were left at specific towns where they stayed for a few weeks while others played cat and mouse with the rioters. The 1st The Queen's Dragoon Guards, for instance had sections in Leeds, Burnley, Blackburn, Otley, Addingham, Manchester and Clitheroe at the end of April. General Sir John Byng reported what was happening in Lancashire and West Yorkshire to the Home Secretary, while his officers reported to him with some of these letters being also sent to London. The tone of much of the correspondence would not have seemed out of place if it had related to the administration of one of the country's colonial possessions when native people were rioting.

The local situation was later summed up by an account in the *Leeds Mercury* on the 6th May 1826, three days after the last of the riots, at a time when those arrested were contemplating their fate in York Castle, others were nursing their wounds and the families of the dead were mourning their loss.

"The outrages which have so much alarmed and disturbed the county of Lancaster, have, we regret to state, extended into this county, and it is not easy to decide whether these outrages have been the spontaneous result of the same mistaken feelings which pervade the operatives of Lancashire, or have been directly excited by emissaries from that county. It is well known that very considerable distress has prevailed for a long time in this district,

but it had been so patiently endured, and so many exertions had been made for its relief, that it was hoped that the public tranquillity would have remained unimpaired. But this expectation has, unfortunately, been disappointed."

Other changes from the early nineteenth century have come about in local government. The growth of industrial areas in the country with small towns, or even villages, becoming large cities necessitated new structures, new ways of funding and administration and new boundaries for each district. The original parishes and Wapentakes, or Hundreds, as divisions of a county, survived until 1894, but other local organisations had by then been established to oversee the financing and delivery of various local services. However, in 1826 the parishes and hundreds as part of a county were still in operation with, for example, the Hundred of East Staincliffe in the West Riding of Yorkshire, including sixteen different parishes. It is difficult now to see the links between Barnoldswick, Burnsall, Keighley, Kettlewell, Skipton, parts of Arncliffe and Addingham, and nine other parishes. The importance for this account though, is that this Hundred was responsible for compensating the owners of machinery destroyed by the rioters. Each parish paid a proportion of the cost.

1825

In February 1825, the festival of the patron saint of woolcombers, Bishop Blaize, was celebrated in style. Manufacturers and workpeople from miles around participated, or watched the procession. Hundreds of people took part, both on foot and on horseback. They included woolstaplers, worsted spinners and manufacturers, wool-sorters, woolcombers and apprentices and masters' sons on horseback. The half-mile procession included several bands and they marched round the main streets of Bradford with flags flying from 10.00 am to 5.00 pm.

This event was one of the few highlights in an era which had seen declining wages since 1812 and more years of suffering which followed. The two growing trades of hand-loom weaving and hand combing had attracted more and more men with the disbanding of the armed forces after 1815 and the movement away from agriculture. Woolcombers separated the long fibres from the short with heavy combs which had to be heated with charcoal. Working conditions were very unpleasant. Apprenticeship restrictions had gone and thousands had been attracted into the trade, as it was a job for men. While some combers worked in large workshops, others worked in small numbers, sharing an independent combing shop. Newcomers often carried on the unhealthy trade in their own homes. Simple combing machines had been introduced, but they could not cope with fine wool and the process was not widely mechanised until the 1850s with much of the development work being done by Samuel Cunliffe-Lister at Low Mill in Addingham, from which he made his first fortune. Certainly the riots in Yorkshire were supported by hand combers, as they feared for their jobs in the same way as the worsted weavers.

The men working on hand looms could be divided into three groups. There was the self-employed weaver who took yarn from a manufacturer and returned a piece of cloth. A journeyman weaver worked either in a loom-shop with perhaps twenty others or in his own home for one manufacturer. The third category was the smallholder who worked part-time at weaving. As the number of weavers expanded, prices for weaving declined with competition for work. Manufacturers who employed the weavers or gave them work exploited this and the price paid for weaving a piece of cloth fell steadily. In areas of West Yorkshire weavers wove worsted or cotton depending on the price paid, but for both fabrics prices went down.

A Skipton correspondent of the *Leeds Mercury* wrote after the 1826 riots that;

> *"From the best information I can collect, the immediate cause of the riots is the extreme low price paid for hand weaving, and the scarcity of work. The price paid to the weaver is such it will not support his family when he is in full work, without parish aid. Calicoes, for which 5s. a piece was paid for the weaving 20 years ago, are now woven in some districts, on the confines of Yorkshire, at 10d. a piece, and 1s. is the maximum price at Addingham, and in this part of the country."*

The writer outlined some of the previous attempts to keep up wages by some of the cotton manufacturers in Blackburn, Burnley, Colne and Todmorden agreeing a price for weaving, which had been supported by many of the buyers. However, there could be a difference of 50 per cent in the wages paid to weave cloth of the same quality by hand, so those who paid the lowest wages could always sell at the lowest price. John Holdsworth, who was convicted of helping attack North Wing Mill in Bradford, was alleged to have said to the Colonel who read the Riot Act that they had to wind, weave, dress and carry home thirty yards of worsted cloth for sixpence (2½ pence).

Two events greatly influenced workers and employers in the area in 1825 and 1826. The first was a twenty-three week strike by wool combers and hand-loom weavers for higher pay. This affected the worsted districts based on

Bradford, Halifax and Keighley, for hand combing and weaving were essential occupations for many and existed alongside work in the established cotton and worsted spinning mills which employed mainly women and children. About 20,000 men stopped work on the 14th June 1825 under the leadership of a wool comber called John Tester. The strike turned into a struggle for union recognition as the Combination Acts had been repealed the previous year. Relations became ugly when the employers dismissed all children working in their spinning mills whose parents refused to sign a document saying they were not in the union. At the beginning of September meetings were held in Halifax and Keighley by the worsted manufacturers from the surrounding areas. Most of those who attended agreed to sack any worker associated with the union. It was said that weavers were earning 25 per cent less than before the start of the French revolutionary wars. The strikers were helped with donations from many parts of the country and these kept them going until the subscriptions to their funds started to diminish. Huge meetings were held at Fairweather Green, on the outskirts of Bradford. The strike for union recognition was seen as crucial throughout the country and up to £20,000 was contributed to the strike funds. Eventually financial support declined and on the 7th November the union was dissolved. Those who could went back to work on the old terms, but many could not obtain employment.

Over the winter of 1825/26, as a trade depression and company failures swept the country, two local businesses collapsed and ruined many of their customers and in turn their workers. Butterworth Brothers, a large firm of textile merchants with premises at Shelf, between Bradford and Halifax, and also a warehouse at Lawrence Lane in London, sold the output of many local cotton and worsted manufacturers. They suspended payments in December 1825 and a Keighley correspondent for the *Leeds Mercury* reported that

"for two days last this town has been greatly clouded by the suspension of payments of Messrs Butterworth. All the manufacturers and shopkeepers, with very few exceptions, are sufferers, and should that house not immediately resume their payments, many must inevitably be ruined."

The textile manufacturers' hand combers and weavers were also put out of work. A local example was John Hanson, a worsted manufacturer in Keighley who had given wool out to combers in Nesfield, across the river from Addingham, who could no longer employ them. The collapse of this large firm of merchants was known as the 'Butterworth Panic' in Keighley, but the hearing for the bankruptcy of Jabez, Joseph and Sidney Butterworth was held in Bradford.

The stock market crash in 1825 was world-wide and the Bank of England had to be helped by the Banque de France. However, it was the collapse of sixty country banks, which affected the local economy, particularly Wentworth & Co. of Low Ousegate in York who drew on Messrs Wentworth & Co. of 25 Threadneedle Street in London. This bank had branches in other Yorkshire towns and its collapse brought down many other firms and tradesmen. The collapse of the Wakefield branch of this bank affected farmers in the East Riding of Yorkshire as well as Lincolnshire and Norfolk who sold corn, wool and cattle and were paid with drafts on this bank. Eventually the partners of Wentworth, Chaloner, Rishworth & Co. paid 20 shillings (100 pence) in the pound on the private debts and were expected to pay 15 shillings (75 pence) on the partnership debts by the end of January, 1827, but by then it was too late for many of their customers.

The weavers had seen some good years until the end of 1825, with plenty of work at times, despite the recent installation of power looms in mills in parts of Lancashire around Manchester. The plentiful supply of yarn from the new spinning mills and improvements to the hand loom at the end of the eighteenth century had brought about a big expansion in trade. In Lancashire and West Yorkshire villages hand looms had been set up in any space that was available. Around Settle, for example, it had been said that

"... the sound of the hand-loom might be heard in every village in the district, and in almost every street. From the town of Settle and the

adjacent villages there must have been a considerable output of hand-made fabrics."

Hand-loom weaving and power-loom weaving existed side by side at this point, but now both trades were suffering because of an excess of supply over demand. Thousands worked at the loom in the Pennine villages as little skill was involved and usually there was no alternative employment. Unfortunately, power looms were not introduced quickly enough, so weavers struggled on until the early 1840s, working harder and harder for smaller rewards.

1826

The slow introduction of power looms meant that over the years thousands of hand-loom weavers lost their livelihood, but this process did not start until there was a serious downturn in trade at the end of 1825. A few months later this led to the riots for four days in Lancashire, followed by those which are the subject of this study.

One important fact to bear in mind is that the processes of specialisation and concentration of the cotton and worsted industries, where we associate cotton with Lancashire and worsted with Yorkshire, were still developing. The division never became as rigid as generally thought. Cotton-spinning mills had been built in the West Riding since 1780 and many, particularly in the Skipton and Craven area, continued until after the Second World War. The first steam-powered mill in Bradford, Holme Mill, was one-third cotton and two-thirds worsted. In 1826 John Knight & Co. were still spinning cotton at their mill in Great Horton, Bradford and there were large numbers of hand-loom weavers engaged in weaving calicos around the town. Though the commentators at the time referred to what was happening in Lancashire cotton towns, the circumstances were also true of areas of Yorkshire. High Mill at Gargrave was filled with cotton machinery and Addingham Low Mill had only recently changed from worsted to cotton. Hand-loom weavers in the area could easily change from weaving one type of yarn to the other and did so depending on the relative price difference.

The *Morning Chronicle* of April 25th 1826 quoted a *Manchester Guardian* account of the situation in Lancashire. It applied equally to Airedale and Wharfedale.

"The state of the poor throughout the whole cotton manufacturing district continues to be most deplorable. Not only is the number who are out of work greater than at any former period within our recollection, but even a large proportion of those who are not wholly destitute of employment are so far from having full work, that the insufficiency of their earnings, during the time they are employed, reduce their families to great distress, whilst, with respect to another large class, the hand weavers, particularly those engaged in the manufacture of calicoes, the rate of payment for their labour is now reduced so extremely low, that even such as have work, can scarcely obtain a pittance adequate to the support of nature. In these observations we wish to be understood as referring, not only to this town, but also to the towns of Blackburn, Colne, Bolton, Burnley, Rochdale, and others throughout the cotton districts."

The hand-loom weavers' riots in Lancashire were far more extensive than those in Yorkshire, and started earlier because more mill owners had already installed power looms. The riots appeared to be a desperate and final reaction to an unbearable situation by starving people. Certainly two forays into Yorkshire were initiated by Lancashire men, but they gathered considerable support along the way. However, in Lancashire the rioting was mainly confined to the north-east of the textile area adjoining Yorkshire, with few disturbances around Manchester

Several factors gave rise to the riots. Firstly, breaking machines, particularly those belonging to unpopular manufacturers, was seen by many workers as their only way of expressing their frustration as they had no political voice and no economic power. Moreover, in early 1826 there was a general depression of trade and thousands were soon out of work and starving. Bad times had regularly seen wages forced down as weavers competed for the little work there was. This happened again with weavers forced to accept less and less for their labour. There were estimated to be over 1,000 paupers around Colne and some farmers were paying more in poor rates than rent. Special subscription schemes were set up in towns and cities to help the destitute, who found workhouses full. Beggars thronged the roads and the middle classes took alarm as insurrection grew more likely. The looms which had been installed, and the hundreds which were in the process of being put to work were seen as the enemy.

Though most looms had been installed in Lancashire towns such as Manchester, Oldham and Bolton, it was the weavers of Rossendale and East Lancashire who came to breaking point at the end of April, 1826. The Pennine weaving villages had grown rapidly since the 1780s. The people who lived there were very self-reliant and behaved predictably when they realised that their existence was about to be destroyed. Several magistrates and clergy were sympathetic to the unemployed weavers. The authorities, such as they were, could only maintain law and order through a combination of the magistrates and the militia. Also, unlike the large towns, there were few alternative sources of work.

After an orgy of loom-breaking in east Lancashire on Monday the 24th of April, more followed on the Tuesday with extra troop reinforcements called for. Help was sought from Yorkshire and on the Monday evening a troop of the Craven Yeomanry left Skipton for Low Mill at Clitheroe under the command of the non-commissioned officers as the officers were elsewhere. They were followed by a party of Dragoon Guards from Leeds to help their Lancashire colleagues. Pitched battles were fought between the rioters and the military, but only if the dragoons were able to guess which mill would be attacked next. Thousands of looms were eventually destroyed in and around Chorley, Helmshore, Haslingden and Bacup. Men and women were killed and several were arrested. The Riot Act was read in many places, but often had little effect as the rioters usually vastly outnumbered the military. These riots in Lancashire led to an incursion into Yorkshire by men from villages around Laneshaw Bridge. However, from the evidence available, it would seem that most of the rioters involved in the attacks at Addingham and Gargrave were local. The riots in Bradford the following week seemed only to involve men from the area, though the authorities thought otherwise.

Rioters starting to break the looms at High Mill, Gargrave

THE YORKSHIRE RIOTS

Monday 24th April

The four days of rioting in east Lancashire started on Monday, 24th April where some form of disturbance had been expected for several weeks. The authorities had made preparations, but not for the scale and intensity of the outburst of feeling. One group smashed looms in mills around Accrington. Another set off for Low Moor Mill near Clitheroe. This was one of the earliest cotton mills in Lancashire, built in 1782, but replaced in 1791 by a five-storey spinning mill with a more recent installation of over one hundred power looms. This was the mill owned by the Garnett and Horsfall families from Yorkshire. The troop of the 1st Kings Dragoon Guards, which had been guarding the mill, were called away, but passed the rioters who were approaching. At this point the officer stopped and warned the mob not to press on. After the officer rode away, men in the crowd told the soldiers they were starving and they were given food from the soldiers' haversacks. The advice to turn round was ignored, but as the mob approached the mill they saw that Jeremiah Garnett had removed anything that could be used as a missile. More seriously, the mill was well barricaded and defended with a cannon and Yeoman Cavalry from the Craven Legion. The mob withdrew, but word was sent by Jeremiah Garnett to his cousin Jeremiah Horsfall in Addingham that his mill would also be attacked. Low Moor Mill, with Yorkshire owners, was the only Lancashire mill where the power looms were not destroyed when threatened by rioters.

Tuesday 25th April
Laneshaw Bridge, near Colne

A heavy cart, pulled by four horses, from a firm of textile machine makers at Newton Moor in Cheshire, was stopped near Laneshaw Bridge on its way to Addingham Low Mill. Local people from the area and nearby villages such as Trawden and Wycoller were looking for any opportunity to break power looms and surrounded the cart. It was carrying spinning mules, not looms, but the crowd did not know that. They threw stones at the driver and unhitched the horses. Men climbed on the wagon, ripped off the cover and uncovered the mules, which they destroyed. The bruised driver returned home with the broken machines, which were valued at more than £100. The news of this destruction added to the fear that Low Mill was likely to be attacked next.

Wednesday 26th April
Addingham

Low Mill at Addingham, built 1787

Jeremiah Horsfall's cousin in Clitheroe, Jeremiah Garnett, whose mill had been threatened on the Monday and Tuesday, found out that rioters were to attack Addingham Low Mill on the Wednesday and immediately gave him this information. On the Wednesday morning he sent a messenger to warn him that the attack was imminent. By that time, the initial group of rioters had set out from Colne, Laneshaw Bridge and the surrounding villages for the thirteen-mile march to Addingham.

We have been informed by a gentleman who arrived from Keighley last night, that a body of from four to five hundred men, were seen to pass from Lancashire to Addingham, to attack the mills there; an express was immediately sent to Mr. Lister, of Manningham, the proprietor. It was expected there would be a sangunary conflict, as although there were no military, the mill was in a complete state of defence, and ready to meet any attack.

Bradford & Huddersfield Courier, 27th April 1826

This information was also sent to Ellis Cunliffe Lister, the owner of the mill, who was in Bradford. It was reported that when the marchers crossed into Yorkshire they numbered from four to five hundred men, although that might have been an exaggeration. However, along the way hand-loom weavers and others joined the marchers at Cowling and villages like Glusburn, Kildwick and Eastburn in the Aire valley, before they climbed over the hill and down through the main street of Addingham to the mill. Kate Mason, in her book *Woolcombers, Worsteds and Watermills*, wrote that they were led by 'Gurt Bill' from Cowling, but that name was not mentioned in any of the newspaper reports. Some men from Keighley also joined the group as did an unknown number from Addingham and in the end they numbered four or five hundred.

The messenger from Clitheroe rode through the rioters just as they were about to approach the village and warned them that he was being followed by one hundred cavalry. He was able to give this message, although false, to the mill defenders, which encouraged them in their defence of the mill. Jeremiah Horsfall, having knowledge of the mules being destroyed the day before, and information from his cousin, had realised that an attack on his mill was planned for that day. He sent his bookkeeper at the mill to William Vavasour of Weston Hall, who was a JP and Deputy Lieutenant of the county, to ask for a defending force to be posted to his mill. As Horsfall was not sure if Vavasour had taken any action, and knowing that the rioters had set off from Colne, he set off on his horse for Leeds to ask for the assistance of the military and left his manager, Timothy Lawson, in charge. Lawson, who had military experience, together with the other men in the mill, had the morning and early afternoon to prepare for the expected attack. They did this by blocking the windows and collecting stones to throw down from the upper floors. In addition some of the defenders were armed with sporting guns and one with an old blunderbuss.

About five o'clock in the afternoon, some having walked thirteen miles from Lancashire, and before Jeremiah Horsfall returned, a mob of four to five hundred people, marched down through Addingham's main street. Only about 150 came near to the mill, but they were armed with hay-forks, cudgels, axes and other weapons and made their way down Low Mill Lane and into the yard at Low Mill. The leaders asked for admittance to smash the power looms, but said they would cause no other harm. This was normal, and in some Lancashire mills all the looms were smashed, but not a window broken. In this case they said that if resistance was offered they would throw all the defenders out of the upper windows. Mr Lawson, the mill manager would not agree, but said he would give them money for their relief, adding that his men were well armed and would defend the mill. The mob decided to go ahead with the attack on the signal from a pistol, fired at the south-west corner of the mill.

The attack on Low Mill

Stones were thrown through the windows and in retaliation missiles were thrown down by the twenty-five men inside the mill. Eventually the windows with their frames and supports were broken and possibly more pistol shots were fired at the defenders. The falling stones did not stop the rioters so after about fifteen minutes shots were fired from within the mill, firstly over their heads and then into the crowd. This went on for some time before Ellis Cunliffe Lister, of Manningham, the owner of the mill arrived, and, as a magistrate, read the Riot Act.

One of the men in the crowd, Edward Marsh, an Addingham weaver, knew one of the defenders, John Parkinson. He shook his fist at him and shouted, *"I know thee, John Parkinson, if we do not kill thee today, we will tomorrow"*. Another defender, Thomas Cowhill, remonstrated with the attackers, but one pulled out a pistol from under his smock and fired at him. The shot missed and in retaliation he fired his blunderbuss, which exploded and took off two of his fingers. Another workman in the mill, John Shepherd, saw an attacker called Henry Town brandishing a wooden stake or hoe. Town was not seen throwing stones, but was shot in the neck and shoulder. He was looked after in Addingham that night and taken home the following day, but later arrested. Another man in the crowd, Anthony Miller, was seen to throw stones and was also arrested later.

Gradually the mob dispersed after the reading of the Riot Act with about twenty wounded. None of Mr Horsfall's men was injured, apart from Thomas Cowhill when his blunderbuss exploded and a few men who were hit with stones thrown through the windows. Nearly all the windows in the mill were broken. As the defenders were using sporting guns with small shot, many of the assailants were struck. Two, who were seriously wounded, were taken back to Colne and eleven were left behind for treatment in the village. Several men were arrested, presumably by special constables who had been sworn in earlier. Three of them, Edward Marsh, Anthony Miller and Henry Town, were later committed to York for trial. John Bannister and William Hartley were also arrested.

Harry Speight, in his book *Upper Wharfedale*, published in 1900, suggested that the householders in Addingham were terrified by news of the impending attack and barricaded their houses or tried to indicate that they were empty by chalking 'for sale' signs on the doors when they knew the rioters were near. How far this true, it is difficult to say. Many of the villagers would have been sympathetic to the unemployed hand-loom weavers as they also worked in the same trade and were themselves suffering. Two local weavers were among those arrested. In addition when several rioters were wounded by buckshot in the attack they were treated in the village before they made their way home. Though a few of the villagers who worked at the mill were involved in defending it, there are no records of clashes between local people and the rioters.

The obvious reason for the attacks on Low Mill, High Mill at Gargrave the next day and North Wing Mill in Bradford the following week was that the introduction of power looms took away work from the local hand-loom weavers. Could there have been a direct link between each mill and a good proportion of those involved in the attacks? This is difficult to prove as no records remain of the weavers who collected yarn from these mills and returned the woven cloth a week later. However, Speight had this to say about the weavers in Addingham.

"Before that time (1822) nearly every cottage had its loom, and in the summer time as you walked down the principal street every door or window was sure to be open, and the continued click-click of the busy shuttle sounded merrily on the still air."

The introduction of the one hundred or so power looms at Low Mill, if multiplied by the number of hand-loom weavers each one replaced, must have resulted in unemployment for several hundreds of local people. Weavers from Addingham were involved with the attack, though the villages around Colne had been a traditional market for the locally-spun cotton yarns from this part of Yorkshire. The attack this Wednesday, and the one the following day, may have been instigated by men from Lancashire, but most of the support was probably fairly local, perhaps involving some of those mentioned by Harry Speight, who lived down the principal street in Addingham, and who were now unemployed and no longer paid to ply the 'busy shuttle' in their own homes.

Leeds

That evening, Henry Whitaker, a son of Jonas Whitaker, a partner at Greenholme Mill in Burley-in-Wharfedale, was staying the night at his uncle's house in Rothwell Haigh near Leeds. His father and uncle had collected him from his boarding school in Leeds for a night with them. About half-past ten in the evening a trooper from the 2nd Dragoons, who were based in Leeds, rode up to deliver a letter. This was from the firm's bookkeeper, who had ridden at haste to the barracks in Leeds to let them know that Jeremiah Horsfall from Low Mill in Addingham had sent word that power-loom rioters were on their way to break his power looms at Low Mill and could then advance to Greenholme Mill to break the 108 cotton power looms which had been installed the previous year.

46

A troop of dragoons had been directed by the magistrates to set off from Leeds for Burley-in-Wharfedale and Addingham and the colonel thought that Mr Whitaker should be informed and so sent one of his men with the letter. Henry's father and uncle promptly set off for the mill at Burley in a gig whilst Henry and his aunt feared very much for their safety as the countryside was full of stories about the destruction of mills and machinery in the cotton-weaving towns and villages of East Lancashire.

Thursday 27th April
Addingham

Five men had been arrested the previous day and were questioned by the local magistrates this morning, Ellis Cunliffe Lister of Manningham, Mathew Wilson of Eshton Hall and William Rhodes of Bramhope. Two were discharged as there was little evidence against them. Anthony Miller, Edward Marsh, both cotton weavers from Addingham, were committed to York for trial at the next assizes together with Henry Town from Eastburn in Airedale. Miller was observed to take an active part in the attack and was reported to have had a fire-arm though that was not true.

Rioters marching down to Addingham Low Mill

By the afternoon a report was received from Cross Hills in Airedale, that one hundred men armed with guns, pikes and pistols were on their way to attack Low Mill again, together with large numbers who had set off from Colne in the morning. The implication of this report is that the rioters came from several villages and probably gathered more on their way to Addingham as happened the day before. However, the previous night F Troop of the 1st Dragoon Guards under the command of Captain Lee and Cornet Fenton had marched from Leeds to Addingham to assist the local magistrates in preventing the rioters from breaking the power looms. The dragoons, who had arrived after midnight, took up positions round the mill and were joined by the magistrates.

In the morning small groups of men approached Low Mill, but retreated when they saw the cavalry. By the afternoon it was estimated that there were several thousand people assembled on the hills around Addingham either waiting to attack the mill or, much more likely, to watch. Those waiting to attack were drawn up in military order about a mile and a half away and were said to be armed with guns, pistols and bludgeons. However, they seemed unsure of what to do in view of the cavalry being stationed round the mill. Mr Lister, the owner of the mill and a magistrate, decided to take action and ordered the commanding officer to send a party of dragoons to frighten the mob and take some prisoners. The dragoons galloped up the road to a small group and two men were arrested by Sergeant Joseph Briscoll as they ran away after climbing over a gate to escape. These two men arrested by the Yorkshire Hussars were on the Skipton Road and were possibly from the group then making their way to Gargrave. One of the men, Hartley Rycroft, was said by the sergeant to have thrown a pistol away before he was captured, but that seems unlikely. The other man was William Walton and they both came from Heyroyd near Colne. A newspaper report said that one of them had a large home-made pistol and the other a quantity of slugs in his pocket. It was said that the barrel of the pistol was about a foot long, but it was held together with a nail and twine. Both were later committed to York Castle for trial. No mention was made of these weapons at the trial so this was probably a rumour to make it look as though the rioters were armed with guns.

Gargrave

The rioters at Addingham had already conferred with each other and decided to withdraw in view of the presence of the soldiers. However, about 200 did not return home immediately, but marched through Skipton in military style to High Mill in Gargrave. On passing through Skipton the numbers grew as the rioters were joined by local men. It was later said by a witness that the men were carrying guns, swords, hammers and pikes. They were met, a short distance from the mill, by the owner, Joseph Mason, who was obviously expecting them as his was the only mill with power looms.

High Mill, Gargrave

By this time it was evening and Mr Mason thought that it was between eight and ten o'clock when he gave his statement to the magistrates a few days later. He offered the men money and attempted to dissuade them from attacking the mill. They rejected his pleas and marched over the bridge and through the village to High Mill where they broke open the door and destroyed the cotton power looms and other machinery in fifteen minutes and then left.

Apart from the mill door there was no damage to the fabric of the mill. Twenty-five power looms were broken as well as twenty-three healds, twenty-two reeds, twenty shuttles and forty pickers, all parts for looms. The rioters also smashed the drive mechanisms to the looms, the belts, shafts and drums, as well as a blower and two warping mills that were used to set up the warp threads on the looms. As the looms had been working, the rioters also destroyed the yarn and the cloth being woven on them.

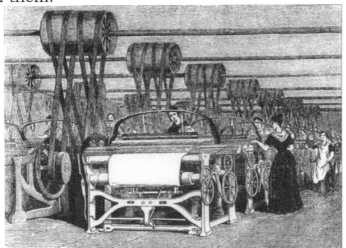

Early Power Looms

Four men were arrested, William Fawcett, William Wade, William Chester and a man named Barker. Evidence against two of them was supplied to the magistrates by George Langstreth, who worked for a man called Hall in

Gargrave. Langstreth was a husbandman, a term at the time for a tenant farmer. That day he had been to Eshton, a hamlet further up Malhamdale, and returned about nine o'clock. When he arrived back in Gargrave he was told that rioters were marching towards the village from Skipton, so he joined the crowd on Gargrave Bridge to wait for them. High Mill in Gargrave is on the other side of the river, so the rioters would have to cross that bridge. After about fifteen minutes the mob arrived armed, he said, with guns and other weapons. They crossed the bridge and went on High Mill. George Langstreth waited a short while and then followed the mob to High Mill where he went inside. There he saw William Chester and Barker breaking up the power looms with a variety of implements. He spoke to Chester and said, "*Well thou's throng at work now, thou was out of a job, but thou's not now*". He also spoke to Barker who had recognised him and asked him how he had arrived there. Chester was a wool-comber and originally from Skipton.

It would appear that the men who joined the group at Skipton were the leaders in breaking the looms. At that time and distance, the group from the Colne area may have already set off home from Addingham. It is difficult to arrive at any conclusion about the numbers and origin of the men who attacked Low Mill at Addingham on the Wednesday and approached the mill again on the Thursday, but then walked several more miles to break the looms at High Mill at Gargrave. Though there were reports of agitators stirring up feelings in

Lancashire prior to the riots there and two men from near Colne were arrested near Addingham, all the others who were identified as being involved lived locally. The disturbances this week and the following week in Bradford, appear to have had strong local support. The few references that exist would support the argument that on both days a significant proportion of the men who took part in the riots at Addingham and Gargrave came from Addingham itself and the Aire valley between Keighley and Skipton. These were essentially local reactions, copying those in Lancashire, to the installation of power looms in local mills which took away work from the hand-loom weavers. Low Mill in Addingham and High Mill in Gargrave were spinning cotton at this time.

Skipton

The town of Skipton was full of activity that evening as there were several textile mills in the town and surrounding villages, though none had power looms. Detachments of the Craven Yeoman Cavalry had already marched to Clitheroe where it was said that thousands of rioters were collecting. The local magistrates swore in large numbers of special constables who arrested a number of people who had marched to Gargrave, but others absconded. Those arrested were examined by the magistrates, but none of them had been committed by the following Wednesday.

Friday 28th April
Addingham

The two weavers from near Laneshaw Bridge arrested on Thursday evening were said to have pistols. Both were remanded on Friday the 28th and underwent a final examination on the Saturday by two magistrates, Ellis Cunliffe Lister and William Rhodes. The men, John Bannister and William Hartley, were not seen rioting, but were committed to York Castle on a misdemeanour charge. There is no record of these men being tried at York, so they were probably released by the magistrates.

Otley

Lieutenant-Colonel Yorke and Adjutant Smith arrived in Otley and the whole regiment received orders to be ready to turn out at short notice. The Ripon Troop of the Yorkshire Hussars arrived in Otley about midnight.

Saturday 29th April
Otley

The Harewood Troop of the Yorkshire Hussars arrived in Otley about 4.00 in the morning. Later fifty men of the Ripon Squadron marched into the town under the command of Cornet Bruce and the mills in the neighbourhood were garrisoned by the Hussars.

Thornton-in-Craven, Skipton

Two clergymen in the area, who tried hard to raise funds for those who were suffering starvation in their parishes, were Rev. Henry Heap in Bradford and Rev. Mordaunt Barnard, the curate of Thornton in Craven and Barnoldswick. They tried to raise money themselves, but also wrote to the Secretary of the Home Department, Sir Robert Peel, for assistance. The following letter was sent by Mordaunt Barnard on April 29th after the riots in Lancashire, and the attacks at Addingham and Gargrave, and explained the situation in parts of the Craven district. This letter was also published in the *Morning Chronicle* and picked up by the *Leeds Mercury* on the 6th of May.

"Sir
As the curate of two miserably distressed Parishes consisting of a population exceeding 6000 I venture to appeal to your consideration on our behalf. The labouring classes depend entirely on cotton weaving for their support. 4/5ths are quite out of work – so many starving – the small farmers are nearly paupers themselves and the larger ones are dreadfully reduced. During the last six weeks we have raised a fund by a private subscription among ourselves by which relief has been weekly extended to upwards of 400 poor families. This is now nearly exhausted and without any prospect of a fresh supply. Though there are disturbances around us, I am happy to say that our population has

taken no share in them. I have weekly visited to the houses in each parish, and have witnessed cases of their most appalling distress. In one parish the carcase of a cow thrown on a dung heap was devoured and in the other with the case of a lying-in woman who had scarcely had any nourishment during 20 hours, and her husband had absolutely nothing. The relief I was enabled to send them is from our fund and preserved this family from starvation.

If there should be any funds within your control which you could apply, however small the amount might be, it should be most gratefully received and faithfully applied. I may perhaps be permitted to add that I have myself submitted to the utmost farthing my limited income ... and that our whole family, including two young gentlemen who are my pupils have agreed to abstain from wine and beer and to apply the saving to the relief of those around us. If this application should be attended with success it will add one more reason to the numerous ones for which I have looked up to you with ... and gratitude.

Your most obedient and faithful servant, Mordaunt Barnard, Curate of Thornton and Incumbent Curate of Barnoldswick
Thornton Rectory, near Skipton-in-Craven. April 29th 1826

The *Leeds Mercury* praised Rev. Mr Barnard for his 'humanity, zeal and intelligence' in raising £140 which had supplied 440 families with oatmeal at half price for the last three months. Now his efforts would enable the relief to continue.

There was then a separate appeal from the Craven area to the Home Office following this one above by Mordaunt Barnard. The second was by a group of four local gentlemen who wrote to the Home Office the following day.

Sunday 30th April
Addingham

Two of the men arrested at Addingham, William Walton and Hartley Rycroft, came from near Heyroyd, a small hamlet on Skipton Old Road near Colne. They were taken to York Castle with a military escort at six o'clock in the evening. They were charged with being concerned in the attack on Low Mill on the Thursday and were later tried on the 10th of July. One troop of the Yorkshire Hussars left their post protecting Low Mill at Addingham for Skipton, but was replaced with a number of men from the 5th Dragoons from Burnley.

Otley

At 8.00 pm, Colonel Yorke, from his temporary headquarters in Otley, sent an order for the Knaresborough troop to be mobilised. Following the events of the Wednesday and Thursday the military remained in the area to prevent further attacks on the mills in Wharfedale. Otley was described as having changed from a quiet market town into an active military station with troops hurrying through to parts of Lancashire.

Craven

Four prominent local men wrote to the Home Office to explain that they intended to form a committee to deal with the distribution of relief funds for the area which *'His Majesty may generously please to give'*. They were Matthew Wilson from Eshton Hall, William Birkbeck a merchant and mill owner from Settle, William Carus Wilson and William Alcock who was a banker and solicitor in Settle. The area they wished to cover included the parishes of Keighley, Kildwick, Thornton and Barnoldswick. They were aware of the great deal of distress in these areas of Craven and strongly recommended the King's support. This letter worried the Rev. Mordaunt Barnard, who had written previously, and he wrote to the Home Office again on the 3rd of May as he did not feel that the four men would distribute the money in a fair and just way.

Monday 1st May.
Addingham

On Monday the 1st of May it was expected that a further attack would be made on Low Mill and people waited for several hours in anticipation. The *Leeds Mercury* correspondent reported however, that such an attack was most unlikely without great bloodshed as the mill was so well defended. He was shown round the mill by Captain William Rhodes from Bramhope, late of the Life Guards and who had been at the battle of Waterloo. Captain Rhodes had been at the mill the previous week and, it was said, had rendered the mill almost impregnable and was in charge of the defenders including the workmen. In addition a troop of the 5th Dragoons and a small detachment of the Craven Legion were stationed by the mill and the village itself was said to be quiet.

There was a great shortage of accommodation for the men and horses of the Dragoons who were stationed in Addingham to resist any further attacks on Low Mill. About twenty of them, under the command of Major Creighton, and the Otley Troop of the Yorkshire Hussars under Captain Lee had to find billets in local farms and barns

Bradford

Thomas Horsfall, the manager at North Wing Mill, had been aware for several days that there was a strong intention to attack his mill following the attacks in Lancashire and at his brother's mill in Addingham. He had spoken to the local magistrates about this and they had promised to assist him should the mill be attacked. He also acquired what arms he could, but these were largely pikes rather than firearms. Special constables had been sworn in, and military aid was made available, though not initially posted at the mill.

During the morning, rumours of a meeting to be held on Fairweather Green, near Bradford, swept through the district and about two hundred and fifty people met there in the afternoon. There were no leaders and no common agreement as to what action to take to relieve their desperate poverty, despite a general feeling of excitement and anticipation among the crowd. They discussed what action to take and decided in the end to move to Horsfall's mill at the other side of Bradford. At about five o'clock they arrived at North Wing Mill and started throwing stones at the windows. They then went to Bradford Moor where they were joined by about two hundred more. With this reinforcement to their numbers they started to move again towards North Wing Mill. Between eight and nine o'clock they arrived at the mill and started to throw stones. Colonel Plumbe Tempest and the Reverend Lamplugh Hird, accompanied by special constables, went to the mill and Colonel Tempest immediately started talking to the mob about the danger of their actions. He explained that breaking the looms would damage the economy of the country and harm the workers in the mill. He asked them to disperse, but they refused and started to stone the windows of the mill again. The two magistrates then read the Riot Act at which point the crowd began to move away and there was no further trouble that night. About 240 panes of glass had been broken, but were replaced the following day together with iron bars to strengthen the frames and some reinforcement was added to the mill doors.

Rev. Hird and Col. Temple read the Riot Act

John Plumbe Tempest lived at Tong Hall outside Bradford and the Reverend Lamplugh Hird lived at Low Moor House not far away. Low Moor, to the south of Bradford, was the site of the large ironworks and Rev. Mr Hird had married into the Hird family who were partners there. He was a wealthy landowner with another living in the East Riding. He also served as deputy-lieutenant of the West Riding.

Skipton
Monday evening

Rumours had spread through Skipton that another attack was to be made on mills at Addingham and that a large group had gathered on Rombald's Moor to plan this. Similarly, nearly ten thousand were supposedly assembling on Colne Moor. The magistrates had asked that all the 'respectable' inhabitants come forward to be sworn in as special constables. Two young men, William Calvert and Richard Ellison, had been held and questioned three times by J N Coulthurst and the Reverend Lister, being charged with the attack on Mr Mason's mill in Gargrave and breaking the looms. They were remanded for another day. Warrants had been issued for the arrest of four others for the same offence.

Joseph Mason, the owner of High Mill, was examined by magistrates in Skipton. He explained that he was in business as a cotton spinner and manufacturer of calico cloth and detailed the damage sustained to the machinery in his mill. He said that he did not know any of the men who attacked his mill.

Otley

The inhabitants of Knaresbro' were alarmed about three o'clock on Monday morning, by the bugle of the Yorkshire Hussars, calling up the members of the corps resident in that town to immediate service. By four o'clock, the troop was in full march towards Otley.

Leeds Mercury, 6th May 1826

Hussars riding through Ilkley

About 3.00 a.m. a bugle had been sounded in the streets of Knaresborough and an hour later part of the Knaresborough Troop of the Yorkshire Hussars left for Otley. A number of them lived near Boroughbridge, but had quickly made their way to Knaresborough. Lieutenant Colonel Yorke marched from Otley at five o'clock in the morning to Ilkley to protect Low Mill at Addingham where an attack was anticipated. As it did not take place the troop set off at three o'clock for Bingley and then over to Baildon where they left a sergeant and twenty men to defend Gill Mill at Tong Park where combing machines had recently been installed. These were seen as creating unemployment for the hand combers of worsted in the same way as power looms made hand-loom weavers redundant. The main body then marched to Bradford, which they reached at eleven at night. The town was in an uproar after the violence that had taken place that day, with, it was later said, the local people assisted by a large number from Lancashire. This mention of assistance from rioters from Lancashire, in a history of the Yorkshire Hussars published in 1853, is one of the very few mentions of any Lancashire influence on the Bradford riots. However, none of the men and boys killed, wounded or arrested came from Lancashire and no-one among the rioters was identified as coming from the county.

There was another report that men had assembled near Bingley early on the Monday morning and set off in military formation, but no-one knew where they had gone, though the same or another group were said to have been seen later on Ilkley Moor.

Thornton in Craven, Skipton

The Rev. Mordaunt Barnard again wrote to the Home Office, and this time his letter was also signed by Christopher Bracewell who was a prominent cotton manufacturer and landowner around Earby and Thornton. They were worried that the four men from other parishes in Craven, who had written about their intentions to form a committee to distribute any funds allocated, would not give the area they represented a fair share. They also added that *'nor have we resident within our parishes any gentlemen of rank and influence enough to urge our claim to its due extent'*. This claim was for the 6,000 or more who lived in the most deplorable situation in their parishes. Most were cotton weavers and most were out of work with no other form of work available. The two men believed that no other area had such a strong a claim as they had. In their two villages people were starving in silence, the small farmers were becoming paupers and the larger ones impoverished. They believed that *'our distress very far exceeds that of the bulk of the population of the district'*. A further reason they had for dealing with any funds was that *'we would therefore feel much more satisfaction in receiving <u>directly</u> from yourself whatever sum you may be pleased to award, and we are morally certain that coming from his Majesty it will afford us all a much superior gratification to that we should feel at its distribution by Gentlemen resident here who cannot but be influenced by local interests and prejudice.'*

Tuesday 2nd May
Leeds

On May 2nd General Harris wrote the following letter to Sir Robert Peel the day after he arrived in Leeds from Lancashire, but before he moved on to check the defences at the local mills.

Sir,
On the arrival of Sir John Byng at Manchester I, according to orders, repaired yesterday into Yorkshire. I think it proper to communicate to you the information received by me respecting the state of the country through which I passed.
At Rochdale some apprehensions were entertained that an attack would be made upon the only power loom mill in that town. I

succeeded in inducing the civil authorities to take steps to defend it and they appeared confident in their means.

At Halifax tranquillity continued to prevail, but in Bradford a considerable number of people were collected on the streets, and an attack upon Mr Horsfall's Mill was anticipated, some recruiting soldiers were armed and placed in conjunction with the workmen in the mills and I have this morning informed that the rioters, upon ascertaining that they would be opposed, deserted after throwing some stones.

On my arrival at Leeds I found that a meeting was expected to take place from which the civil authorities anticipated little danger, but a very few persons attended, they departed quietly.

This morning I had an interview with the mayor and magistrates of this town and I am happy to say they have great confidence in the prevailing peaceable disposition of the working classes.

From what I have seen it is evident that the civil authorities here are extremely vigilant and have better information respecting those inclined to engage in this combination than has generally been the case. From these statements I have reason to suppose that the disorder will be prevented from starting. News which must be gratifying to you.

I shall only add that the owners of factories here, are preparing to defend their property, and in order to induce them do so, the recruiting parties stationed in the town are

armed and ready to aid those within the mills, as a very few soldiers appears to infuse the workmen with every requisite confidence.
It may be necessary to mention that my head-quarter is at Wetherby.

I have the honour to be
Sir
Your most obedient Humble servant, Harris,
Maj. General

There had been a meeting on Monday evening on Hunslet Moor, but the crowd had dispersed. Another small group assembled in the same place that evening and again dispersed, but later about 300 'operative manufacturers' met in Briggate and marched to Stanfells' mill on Kirkstall Road where power looms had been installed. Soldiers had guarded the mill for several days and the mob having arrived without weapons, gave a few cheers and returned home. There were other alarms in Leeds over several days, but no violence occurred. The reason, as the *Leeds Intelligencer* reported, was that *"... a steady, vigilant eye is kept, by our local authorities, upon the proceedings of the lower orders."* The presence of the Leeds troop of the Yorkshire Hussars and a detachment of the 5th Dragoon Guards in the local barracks no doubt also helped.

Burley-in-Wharfedale

Fears grew in Burley-in-Wharfedale that Greenholme Mill would be attacked. General

Harris, who had been planning the defence of the mill villages and towns around Manchester, arrived in the village about 2.00 p.m. on Tuesday afternoon and spoke to local magistrates before driving to Low Moor Mill near Clitheroe in a post chaise to examine the defences at Garnett & Horsfall's mill. He took with him an officer and several soldiers from the Dragoon Guards who had been stationed at Burley. Lord Grantham and other officers arrived from London and the Leeds Squadron under Captain Becket joined them in Bradford to make up the complete regiment. The following day Captain Beckett, Lieutenant Brooke, two sergeants, two corporals, a trumpeter and thirty privates marched to Halifax to relieve F Troop under Captain Lee who returned to their homes.

London

The Lord Mayor of London chaired a meeting on Tuesday 2nd May *"for the purpose of raising a subscription to alleviate the pressure of suffering which weighs so heavily upon the manufacturing classes of the north."* The *Morning Chronicle* described the gathering as *"one of the most imposing assemblies we have ever witnessed"*, based on the rank, wealth and numbers of those present. They included the Archbishop of Canterbury, the Bishop of London, the Home Secretary Sir Robert Peel, leading politicians and bankers. Also present was Dr George Birkbeck, representing the artisans in the distressed areas. Born in Giggleswick, near

Settle, to a Quaker family of merchants, bankers and textile mill owners, he was the first president of the London Mechanics' Institute which he helped found in November 1823. Among the sums distributed initially was £500 for Settle and neighbourhood, £200 for Gargrave and neighbourhood and £500 for Thornton, Barnoldswick and neighbourhood. These were the only sums allocated to Yorkshire manufacturing areas. The coincidence of Dr Birkbeck's presence at the meeting and the money given to help the starving hand-loom weavers around Settle is interesting. The earlier appeal from the Rev. Barnard Mordaunt for help to be distributed to the starving hand-loom weavers around Thornton and Barnoldswick in Craven also shows how his initiative was soon rewarded.

To help the committee, applicants filled in forms with eleven detailed questions. These ranged from basic queries about the population of the town or village, the usual employment in the area, the various proportions of people employed and unemployed to the measures taken to provide employment. More detailed questions were asked about the existing poor rate and the prices of bread, oatmeal, meat, cheese and fish. In the following weeks local committees were set up and submitted appeals, resulting in allocations of money to various parts of the country, including Yorkshire. Local and national newspapers printed the details.

Bradford

An anonymous notice requested the wool-combers and stuff weavers of Bradford and the surrounding area to meet on Fairweather Green the following day.

Public Meeting on Fair Weather Green

At the suggestion of some of our employers, we, the woolcombers and stuff weavers of Bradford and its vicinity, hereby convene a meeting on Fairweather Green, on Wednesday, the 3rd of May 1826, at one o'clock, to take into consideration the present unparalleled distress and famishing state of the operatives, and if possible, to devise some prompt and effectual means to afford them relief.
A numerous attendance is particularly requested

Leeds

Lord Grantham, the commandant of the Yorkshire Hussars, and other officers arrived from London.

Wednesday 3rd May
Bradford

According to the local paper it was well known in the town that a second attack on North Wing Mill was imminent. At three o'clock in the afternoon the Yorkshire Hussars were ordered to defend John Horsfall's mill. Ten men took up positions in the mill together with about twenty soldiers from the recruiting service in Leeds under Lieutenant Richard Fry from the 63rd Regiment.

Initially, the meeting at Fairweather Green advertised the previous day was sparsely attended, and again there were no leaders and no agreement as to what action to take, apart from a suggestion to present a petition to Parliament for the repeal of the Corn Laws, which made food very expensive. Reports said that about 1,000 people did collect, but had little idea of what to do and there were no speeches. Eventually, just after three o'clock, the people moved towards Bradford and then, in separate groups walked to the mill belonging to John Garnett Horsfall & Co, which was on the other side of the town. The editor of the *Bradford & Huddersfield Courier*, Henry David Inglis, who saw them march past his office, followed them. In his estimation there were about 1,500 men, many of them armed with bludgeons.

Henry Inglis follows the rioters through Bradford

They arrived about 3.45 pm and assembled on the north side but found it easier to attack the mill from the east side which gave them the advantage of rising ground on a level with the windows. John Ingham, a special constable, had just enough time to lock the mill gates and run into the mill before the attack began. The mob immediately started throwing stones at the windows. Some of the crowd were digging up stones whilst others threw them. One of those digging for stones and then breaking them for others to throw was John Holdsworth, a calico weaver. He was encouraging men to break in through the broken windows from which many of the iron stanchions were wrenched to provide a way into the building. Ingham also estimated that there had been at least 1,500 people in the crowd round the mill, but only about 200 to 300 were throwing stones.

Inside the mill were about forty defenders, ten chosen by the mill manager, Thomas Horsfall, and the thirty armed soldiers. The men inside the mill had been given defensive positions and Thomas Horsfall went round checking on the situation as the barrage of stones continued. Some men were hit, but none seriously. Some stones were flung with such force that they went out of windows on the opposite side. When Horsfall was asked later if he was frightened, he said he was not, as he was confident that they would repel any attack though if entry had been gained there probably would have been loss of life. The attackers made no demands and he had no chance to reason with them. Colonel Tempest and Thomas Horsfall ordered the defenders not to fire unless there was an attempt to enter the mill.

Inglis, who had followed the mob to North Wing Mill stood on a wall to get a better view and saw the rioters attack both sides of the mill with stones. Then one man tried to remove the stanchions at a lower window. The firing then started without warning, much to his surprise, so he hid behind the wall he had been standing on. At that point the magistrates had not arrived at the mill and the Riot Act had not been read. In all the attack lasted about twenty minutes and many of the rioters were driven off before the magistrates came.

When it looked as though men were about to climb through a window opening, the defenders had opened fire, apparently directly at the crowd and about thirty shots were fired.

The crowd thought these were blanks, fired as a warning, but were soon proved wrong. Jonas Bairstow from Queen's Head (Queensbury), who was eighteen, was the rioter attempting to enter the mill through a window opening. He saw one of the soldiers inside the mill raise his gun to shoot at him and turned to run, but was shot in the back. The shot went through his lungs and out of his chest and as a result he died that night. Henry Fearnley, from Bradford, who was thirteen years old and also shot, died on the Thursday night. Others wounded and taken to the dispensary were William Walker, aged 22 from Baildon, who was shot through the right arm from one of the upper storeys of the mill, the ball entering his right side, Charles Wilson from Halifax who was shot in the chest with the ball remaining in his body, John Milner from Great Horton, wounded in the thigh, William Briggs aged 17, from Bingley, shot in the arm, John Barker a weaver from Clayton, aged 16, shot through the wrist and John Taylor aged seven, wounded in the groin. The boy had gone

Workhouse children

to see what was happening on his way home from school to the workhouse in which his mother was an inmate. Thirteen-year-old Henry Fearnley from Church Bank, Bradford, the son of a joiner was shot, but went home.

Amongst the crowd was Titus Salt who was later to build his famous mill and village at Saltaire. An early biographer of his mentioned his sympathy with working people and that an eye witness had seen him mingling with the rioters taking – *"an active part in trying to bring the malcontents to reason; he went into the very thick of the mob, and was not frightened a bit; he remonstrated and reasoned with them, but all in vain."* The same eye-witness later saw Titus Salt working for the establishment of law and order. *"I remember seeing William Rand (local mill owner's son) and Titus Salt hurrying up and down, trying to induce their fellow-townsmen to come forward as special constables."* Titus Salt was twenty-three years old at the time. About two months later William Rand was one of the secretaries responsible for distributing relief to the poor in Bradford.

At half past four Colonel Tempest with the Rev. Lamplugh Hird, Ellis Cunliffe Lister and Timothy Horsfall, again accompanied by special constables, arrived at the mill. At that point some rioters started to run away, but Colonel Tempest held up his staff to get attention and standing on ground nearby read the Riot Act. This had little effect on the reduced crowd who continued throwing stones. John Holdsworth, a calico weaver, who was later arrested, told Colonel Tempest how little he could earn and asked, *"should I go home and starve?"* The colonel replied that he was sorry for his condition and that if he would see him tomorrow he would help him, but if the riot continued it would lead to very serious consequences. Eventually the stone throwing slowed, but the people did not disperse so two troops of the Yorkshire Hussars from the 73rd Regiment, led by Lord Grantham and Colonel York, were requested from Leeds. The soldiers, together with the special constables, scattered the crowd, but not before James Crawley from Bradford was arrested for throwing a stone at Captain Smith. The military within the mill were ordered by the magistrates to return to their quarters. They were replaced by the 73rd Regiment and within a few days returned to the peaceful environment of Harewood Park.

Later that evening William Bolton from Mill Hill in Bradford and John Holdsworth from Clayton were arrested, taken to the Talbot Inn, and questioned by the three magistrates, Colonel Tempest, the Reverend Lamplugh Hird and E C Lister. The two prisoners were charged with attempting to destroy North Wing Mill and machinery. Holdsworth's statement was that *"if the Almighty were to strike me dead at this moment, I did not throw a single stone nor was I there with that intent."* James Gledhill, a labourer from Bradford, said that he saw Holdsworth throw stones and that he was very active in the riotous assembly.

Samuel Ingham, a labourer and special constable, said that the mob had been trying to destroy the mill and the machinery in it. He had seen William Bolton with a stick in his left hand and throw stones with his left hand. When he was near the mill he threw the stick away and *"began encouraging the mob in acts of violence"*.

Bolton and Holdsworth were sent to York Castle with a military escort that night. Two others who were arrested were dismissed for lack of evidence.

During the night the town was patrolled by special constables and when they reported to the magistrates after midnight, they were able to inform them that the town was quiet including the area round Horsfall's Mill. A squad of infantry, made of detachments from different regiments, and commanded by an officer, arrived from Leeds to reinforce the recruiting staff defending the mill. The officer, whose name is difficult to read, wrote the following letter to Sir John Byng that evening.

Bradford May 3rd 1826

My Dear Sir John
We had an attack on the mill some way after the meeting at Fairweather Green (which was quite insignificant) and no speaking. They attacked with volleys of stones and attempted to break in, it is also said that some shots were fired, but I cannot ascertain if they were mainly shouting at our window, when after being warned they were fired upon from within. 7 people were wounded, 2 very severely (1 it is said now dead). 2 prisoners were taken and have been sent to York Castle. A small supply of infantry from the recruiting staff has been stationed here this evening to support and relieve the men in the mill, but the officer commanding the further detachment that was here before this evenings reinforce-

ments, thought his force so weak that I let him have 10 men who were in it when attacked.

A magistrate from near Addingham reports today that all is quiet there. I have determined on sending another troop to Otley in the morning and Capt. Beckett, who is at Halifax, reports that as there is not a single infantry soldier there and numerous applications for help to defend mills are made he thinks his detachment of 30 men too weak to remain long there without reinforcements. I have ordered Sergeant Major Petrie from Leeds with the part of the Regiment which I had halted there and I expect this in the morning.

I remain, my dear Sir John, Yours truly, (Name and rank) Yorkshire Hussars

The officer states that the rioters were warned before being fired on, but all the eye witness accounts deny that.

Craven

As the following letter to the Home Office explains, the vicar of Thornton in Craven had been able to settle his differences with the local group of gentlemen that had been set up to distribute funds raised by the London Committee. The mention of 'half a bank note' was a way of avoiding theft as the other half would be sent separately.

Sir,

I have the honour with the most grateful thanks to acknowledge the receipt of one half of a bank note of £50 from his Majesty towards the relief of the poor of Thornton & Barnoldswick. I have to apologise for troubling you with a letter two days ago to request that our share of His Majesty's £500 might be forwarded immediately from yourself. I have since that time seen the magistrates and gentlemen to whom the distribution will be entrusted to have reason to believe that their arrangements will give satisfaction. I have the honour to be, Sir, your most obliged and obedient servant. Mordaunt Barnard, Curate of Thornton.

Thornton Rectory, near Skipton-in-Craven. May 3rd 1826

Thursday, 4th May
BRADFORD

Magistrates' Meeting

The special constables who had been patrolling the streets of Bradford following the riot and during the night again reported to the magistrates. They met at the Talbot Inn in Bradford on Thursday morning for the examination of other men charged with being involved in the rioting the previous day. James Crawley, a woolcomber from Bradford, had been seen by Robert Gamble, a labourer and special constable, to throw a stone at an officer of the Hussars after the Riot Act had been read. Crawley was sent to York Castle in a chaise, escorted by a detachment of the Yorkshire Hussars. Richardson Williamson was also charged with riotous conduct, but was discharged after being bound over to keep the peace. Two other prisoners who were wounded were remanded for further examination. One was William Walker from Baildon. He had been seen to pick up a stone by John Ingham, a special constable, but was shot before he could throw it at the windows. Ingham later identified him when he was still in the dispensary recovering from his wound.

Coroner's Inquest

The coroner's inquest into the death of James Bairstow, who had died the previous night as a result of being shot, was held at the White Horse Inn. The coroner was James Wrigglesworth and the twelve men in the jury were from Bradford, Great Horton, Bolton and Bowling. They visited the scene of the riot at North Wing Mill and saw the bodies of the two dead rioters. Eighteen-year-old Bairstow who was able to speak until he died, had explained that he had gone with the mob from Fairweather Green to Mr Horsfall's mill where he had helped with the attack. When he was breaking a window with a pole he saw someone about to fire at him. He tried to escape, but was shot in the back. John Walker Roberts, the apothecary at the dispensary gave evidence, as did Thomas Horsfall the mill manager.

Horsfall explained that he had been alerted some days previously to the likelihood of an attack and had been entrusted with its defence. The local magistrates had promised assistance and he had collected some arms for the defence of the mill, mainly pikes. When he saw the mob approaching the mill he ordered the defenders to their previously assigned positions. About ten of them were from the mill, another ten were dragoons and about twenty were from the recruiting staff in Leeds. He admitted that he didn't see any of the rioters carrying arms or sticks, but that a furious attack by stone throwing began as soon as the mob approached the mill. The rioters didn't ask to enter the mill and nothing was said to them as the stone throwing was so violent. He couldn't have spoken to them without risking his life. When there was a shout that men were breaking into the mill, firing commenced as arranged. Horsfall thought that about thirty shots were fired and that the guns were loaded with ball. He admitted that the Riot Act had not been read before the firing started, as there was no magistrate at the mill.

Another witness, Mary Blakey, who lived near the mill, passed by when she was going home from work. She saw Bairstow shot when he was a short distance from her. He wasn't doing anything and didn't have anything in his hands. After he was shot Bairstow did not fall, but was able to walk to the house of John Rhodes. The next witness, Henry David Inglis, the editor of the *Bradford Courier,* had been about thirty yards from the mill. He outlined what he had seen until the firing started, which he did not expect as no warning was given. He then hid behind the wall he had been standing on.

John Ingham, a special constable, had seen Bairstow wrenching the stanchion of one of the windows from its fastening which would have made it easy to enter the mill. He added that the soldiers were not willing to be murdered, which seemed likely. When asked the names of those who fired on the rioters, he said that he was not prepared to say and the question was not asked again. Ingham repeated that they had strict orders not to throw a stone or fire on the assailants unless they were attempting to actually break into the mill.

Joseph Pearce, a sergeant in the 33rd Regiment of Infantry, had been in the mill and considered that they would have been massacred if the mob had got in. The soldiers were under orders not to fire until an attempt was made to enter the mill.

One of the jury, Jeremiah Haley from Great Horton, said that the firing had been too indiscriminate and had gone on too long.

The Jury's verdict was that James Bairstow

"had been shot by some persons to the jurors unknown, in the mill of Messrs. John Garnett Horsfall & Co. in the preservation of the lives of the persons and property therein."

A similar verdict, on similar evidence, was returned in the case of Edward Fearnley, the thirteen-year-old boy, who was shot on the same occasion.

Addingham

Major Crichton, of the 5th Dragoon Guards, was stationed at Addingham and wrote to General Harris, who was staying in Wetherby, to inform him of the situation in the mill villages. It is interesting to read his interpretation of the events, for when he wrote the letter at 11.00 in the morning he had obviously received some news from Bradford and included other information, some of which was not strictly true. He said there had been no further disturbance at Addingham or Burley. William Rhodes, the magistrate, had asked him to see if ten infantry or dismounted dragoons could be stationed at Addingham to relieve the troops there. The magistrates in Burley had not asked him for the same changes, but he saw the situations as being similar as the mill owners had both rendered them more capable of resisting an attack.

He went on to say that, *"Two men were shot at Bradford yesterday afternoon, but I am informed there was not a very violent attack on the mill there, though considerable commotion in the town."* The two men, as we know, were aged eighteen and thirteen.

Major Crichton had also spoken to William Rhodes about the men arrested following the attack at Addingham. The two local men were found to be in *"good circumstances for their position in life"* and only one of them had asked for Parish relief and that had been some weeks previously. One was a pensioner with no family (presumably with a military pension) and the other was an ostler or stable-man at a local inn. Of the two men from Lancashire, the man said to have a gun had thirty shillings in his pocket (£1.50). At their trial a few weeks later there was no mention of a gun or of the money. The idea that the rioters were not men at starvation level, had also been passed on to the major by J N Coulthurst, the magistrate from Gargrave. He had *"agreed to the circumstances of those who destroyed the mill at Gargrave."* As we know the mill was not destroyed or even damaged, only the door broken, twenty-five power looms and some other machinery. There was no hint at any time that the fabric of the building was harmed. These remarks on the circumstances of the arrested rioters throw up some interesting questions about the attitude of the various people commenting on the incidents.

This letter was forwarded to Robert Peel by General Harris, who had received a request for information regarding the disturbances. He had to apologise for not being able to give more information, but had passed all the letters and requests he had received for military help to General Sir John Byng. The requests had been received from Lancashire and Addingham on the 28th, 29th and 30th April. The letter from Major Crichton was obviously intended to illustrate the current situation regarding *"Addingham, Otley and the vicinity where tranquillity appears to be in a great measure restored"*. One concern must be, that if the details and views expressed in Major Crichton's letter were accepted as fact by the Home

Secretary, any future government policy could have been based on incorrect information.

Saturday 6ᵗʰ May

The Vicar of Bradford writing to the Home Secretary

The Bradford magistrates took evidence from John Ingham, a special constable, regarding the attack on North Wing Mill. This was then sent to the Home Secretary. On the same day Henry Heap, the vicar at Bradford, also wrote to Sir Robert Peel for financial help for his starving parishioners. His letter, quoted below, is quite long, but it gives a picture of a humble man, unused to writing begging letters, having to resort to a mixture of flattery and the facts to state his case. He mentions hundreds of people from Lancashire coming, to stir up trouble and inciting the local textile workers to riot. This was also mentioned in the *Leeds Mercury*, published that morning, but is difficult to substantiate. Apart from the two men from near Colne who were arrested a mile or so from High Mill at Addingham on the Wednesday of the previous week, all the others arrested, wounded or killed were local. Certainly the reports about the preliminary meetings before the attacks on North Wing Mill strongly suggested that there were no leaders, no-one was inciting the crowd to violence and even during the rioting only local men were involved. We must also remember that Bradford in 1826 was a small town surrounded by villages and other townships. For instance when John Garnett Horsfall bought the land to build his house, Bolton Royd on Manningham Lane about 1830, it was set in 35 acres and was quite separate from Bradford. Places such as Clayton and Great Horton where two of the rioters came from, were seen as outside Bradford so Henry Heap could claim that most of the rioters came from a distance even if it was Bingley and Queensbury. A later report in the Bradford paper mentioned that it was to the credit of the inhabitants of the Bradford that none of the men came from the town, but from the surrounding villages. As the riot was about the anger of the hand-loom weavers at their livelihood being taken away by the introduction of power looms, that would have been true. The villages round Bradford were largely inhabited by hand-loom weavers and hand combers at the time and hand weaving continued there, though on a declining scale, for many more years.

Sir,

I trust you will pardon the liberty I am taking in addressing you. I am encouraged by your praiseworthy and noble intentions in so promptly and efficiently noticing cases of distress among the poor in manufacturing districts; to lay before you a few particulars respecting the state of things here. In the midst of the great and unparalleled suffering of my poor and unemployed parishioners, which have continued now for many months, no mischievous or turbulent disposition manifested itself before this week. On the contrary, the poor were thankful for the benefits afforded them, and particularly grateful for the liberal subscriptions which were raised by their neighbours to relieve their truly <u>urgent necessities</u>, and had it not been for the ingress of <u>hundreds of strangers</u> from the disturbed parts of Lancashire, I believe the population here, not withstanding their privations, would have continued in order and peace, and any attempt to destroy the power looms would not have existed. I am able to say, from personal observation, that the bulk of the people who assembled in this town on Wednesday last, for the purpose of breaking machinery, were persons not belonging to this Parish, but from a distance. It is true that in all neighbourhoods thoughtless characters will always be found, but I can state from experience that the inhabitants from this town and neighbourhood are particularly <u>loyal and peaceable</u> people and I sincerely hope they will ever continue so. At present the town is *perfectly tranquil and I trust the poor are fully convinced that insubordination is the way to injure themselves and altogether to destroy commiseration for their distresses. But it is absolutely necessary that their wants shall be supplied. We cannot suffer them to perish in their poverty. <u>Much</u> has been done here since the middle of January last by a subscription which was then provided by certain individuals. Weekly aid was forthwith given to 1,050 families, but distress so much abounds that at the end of March 2,300 families obtained a weekly supply of oatmeal. It was then found necessary to make a <u>second</u> subscription as the number of the poor increased and we were also obliged to <u>limit</u> the relief to families whose incomes from all sources did not exceed <u>one shilling</u> weekly for each member of the family. At first the relief was given to all families, whose weekly incomes were under <u>two shillings</u> a head, but if this scale was to be readopted, and <u>had we the means, we should do so</u>, then the number of families claiming relief would not be much short of 3,000. The subscriptions have amounted to upwards of £2,000, but we have <u>nearly</u> exhausted our funds, and I fear without some foreign aid, that an adequate future supply cannot be obtained. I inform you that here <u>all classes</u> are suffering exceedingly, and the great depression in trade brings upon the population injuries of a very <u>serious nature</u>, and if some help cannot be procured for the poor, from some other quarter, the greatest misery must ensue. Very thankful* *shall I be, if after reading this statement you would be pleased kindly to notice the state of this town to our beloved and <u>Revered Sovereign, whose Condescension and Munificence are already so superlatively manifest</u>, and which have so justly earned the love and attachment of his admiring people, and if some pecuniary aid should be forwarded to Bradford, whilst my poor Parishioners would rejoice on receiving the <u>royal bounty</u>, your services on their behalf would, I believe, never be forgotten.*

I have the honour to be, Sir, your humble and obedient servant.

Henry Heap. Vicar. Bradford

Knaresborough

It was reported in the *Leeds Mercury* that effectual precautions against rioting had been taken in Knaresborough the previous week. This had initially taken the form of a survey of the town by the Rev. Andrew Cheap, the vicar, and Dr Murray. They found about 450 families with 1800 men, women and children in need of help. 200 of the families had some work, but 250 had no work and no wages. A committee of local gentry and 'respectable inhabitants' raised £300 to help the unemployed. Knaresborough was a centre for the linen industry with hundreds of linen weavers living and working in the town and nearby villages working with linen yarn spun in the mills nearby.

Monday 8th May
Bradford

About 10.00 in the evening a large detachment of the Yorkshire Hussars under the command of Colonel Geshe arrived to be quartered in the town.

Tuesday 9th May
Bradford

The Leeds troop of the Yorkshire Hussars commanded by Captain Beckett arrived in Bradford about 5.30 pm as did Lord Grantham, their colonel.

Keighley and Skipton

A correspondent from Keighley reported that everything was quiet in the town and neighbourhood. The King's donation of £1,100 was to be distributed in Keighley, Skipton, Gisburn, Thornton (in Craven) and Barnoldswick, together with the £500 raised in London. A troop of the Yorkshire Hussars from Skipton was diverted from the town to Halifax rather than Bingley and a unit of the Craven Legion Yeomanry left for Skipton with a great deal of bad feeling between the Yeomanry and the townspeople.

> The Craven Yeomanry Cavalry, commanded by the Hon. Thomas Lister, commence their permanent duty on Thursday, at Skipton, instead of York, as was originally intended.

Leeds Mercury, 6th May 1826

Harewood

The Hussars assembled in Harewood Park and were inspected by Lieutenant-Colonel Wallace of the 5th Dragoon Guards, after which they had lunch provided by the Earl of Harewood. Flattering letters were received by Lord Grantham, their commanding officer, from Robert Peel, the Home Secretary, Sir John Byng, Major General Harris and Lieutenant-Colonel Maxwell Wallace regarding the high conduct of the regiment during the arduous period of duty they had undertaken.

Wednesday 10th May
Bradford

The Leeds troop of the Yorkshire Hussars left for Halifax. A fund to help the poor in Bradford had been started with donations being taken at the Sun and Talbot Inns where merchants and other visitors could sign a book. Before leaving Bradford, Lord Grantham, on behalf of the regiment, deposited £100 with Messrs Harris's bank to be distributed to the poor in the towns and villages where they had seen stationed.

Friday 12th May
London

The London Committee, with the Archbishop of York in the chair, allocated £300 for the relief of the poor in Otley, Guiseley, Baildon, Menston and Burley-in-Wharfedale.

Saturday 13th May

The vicar of Bradford wrote the following letter to Sir Robert Peel.

Vicarage, Bradford, Yorkshire
May 13th 1826
Sir
I was favoured with your good intentions towards my poor parishioners yesterday. The letter would have reached me sooner, but it travelled round by Bradford, Wiltshire. I sincerely in the name of the inhabitants, but especially of the poor of this town and neighbourhood beg to present to you our united thanks for your valuable services in procuring so liberal a pecuniary supply for alleviating the distresses of the unemployed artisans at Bradford. I trust they will ever retain the most heartfelt gratitude for the subscribed relief now provided for them. All is here perfectly tranquil. Your suggestion shall be attended to.

I have the honour to be, Sir, with high regards, your obliged humble servant. Henry Heap

20th May

It was reported that Henry Town had been committed to York Castle for his part in the attack on Low Mill at Addingham.

Tuesday 23rd May
Keighley

A survey in Keighley showed that out of 6,691 operatives visited, 4,524 had no work and the rest were only partially employed, none of them for more than three days a week

Wednesday 31st May

The three Bradford magistrates wrote to Sir Robert Peel and dated the letter 31st May though it may have been sent a few days later. They enclosed copies of the depositions or statements taken when the three men arrested after the riot on the 3rd May were questioned before being sent to York Castle. They stated ...

> *"We have found the arrangements of the military force, as ordered by Sir John Byng, of the greatest use, and in our opinion, until the trade of this part of the country, and of the adjacent counties of Lancashire and Cheshire, be considerably improved and full employment found for the lower classes of the people it will be absolutely necessary that troops should remain where the late disturbances have taken place."*

The magistrates went on to comment about the attacks and precautions regarding possible future attacks, suggesting that besides power looms, mills were being attacked because they had combing machines. Certainly the 1825 strike involved hand combers as well as hand-loom weavers and combers were involved with the attacks which did occur, but I found no mention of machine wool combs being destroyed. It was felt that the attacks on the mills had been so sudden that neither civil nor military help could reach them in time, so permanent military guards should continue. However, they would not recommend a military guard where the mill owners with power looms or combing machines had not made their own defensive preparations. Combing machines were being introduced slowly and were not very satisfactory.

Saturday 3rd June

The latest grants allocated to towns and villages in Yorkshire by the London Committee were:

Kirkstall, near Leeds	£50
Darton, near Barnsley	£50
Halifax - Elland and Greetland	£200
Skipton – various townships	£1,000
Bingley	£100
Bradford – Heaton	£150
Fewston, near Knaresborough	£50
Denby, near Penistone	£50
Dewsbury and Ossett	£100

Wednesday 7th June
BRADFORD

William Walker from Baildon, who had been wounded in the attack on North Wing Mill, though still a patient in the Bradford Dispensary, was questioned by Bradford Magistrates and bailed to later appear for trial at York Assizes. Two securities were provided. After an appeal to Messrs Horsfall at North Wing Mill and in consideration of the wounds he had received he was released on his own guarantee of £200 and £100 from five "respectable" householders.

A further link between the attacks on Low Mill in Addingham and North Wing Mill in Bradford, comes from the activities of Ellis Cunliffe Lister. As the owner of Low Mill, and a magistrate, he had read the Riot Act when that mill was attacked on the 26th of April. The following day he was there again and ordered the arrest of some of the potential rioters. As he had moved from Addingham to Bradford, and lived at Manningham Hall, he was also involved in questioning some of those arrested for attacking North Wing Mill the following week.

The *Bradford & Huddersfield Courier* carried a list of sixty grants made by the London Committee to the distressed areas. These ranged from £1,000 for Rochdale to £30 for the township of Hoyland, near Halifax. Other Yorkshire recipients were :

Around Halifax -

Norland	£100
Stainland	£150
Stansfield and Langfield	£250
Northowram, Ovenden, Shelf, Clayton and other places	£300
Midgley	£100
Hoyland	£30
Cross-Stone, near Halifax	£300.

Around Bradford and Keighley –

Haworth	£200
Thornton, near Bradford	£300
Shipley	£200
Heaton	£150
Grindleton, near Clitheroe	£50
Earls-Heaton, near Dewsbury	£100
Saddleworth	£250
Fewston, near Knaresborough	£50.

Saturday July 8th
York

The *York Herald* gave the names of the fifteen persons who would be tried at the Yorkshire Summer Assizes starting the following Saturday. Among the accused were seven men to be tried for rioting. They were to be tried before Sir James Allan Park and Sir John Hullock. The first four were indicted for riotously and tumultuously assembling, with above 50 others on the 27th April and beginning to demolish a mill belonging to Jeremiah Horsfall. They were Edward Marsh, 34, Anthony Miller, 19, Hartley Rycroft, 27, and William Walton, 28. One other person tried for his part in the Addingham riot was Henry Town, whose name did not appear on the list. The other three were John Holdsworth, William Bolton and James Crowley who were involved with the Bradford riot.

Monday July 10th
York

The first person to be brought before the court was William Walton who was asked to plead. He stood silent so a jury was sworn in to decide if he was wilfully deciding not to speak. The jailer said that Walton had been in his custody since the 1st of May and he believed him to be insane. On this evidence the jury returned a verdict that he was mute by act of God. It was ordered that he should be handed over to his friends, one of whom said that he had become insane the previous December and both his parents had been of unsound mind.

Hartley Rycroft was then indicted for having, in company with several others, riotously assembled at Addingham, on the 27th April, with the intention of destroying power looms belonging to Jeremiah Horsfall. The prosecution was led by Mr Blackburne and Mr Milner, who questioned the first witness, Ellis Cunliffe Lister. He said that he was a Magistrate for the West Riding and on the morning of the 27th April he went to Jeremiah Horsfall's mills, which had been threatened with an attack. With him was a small group of cavalry. Later that morning a few small groups of men had approached the mill, but retreated when they saw the cavalry. However, in the afternoon he saw several thousand men approaching armed with guns, pistols and bludgeons and marching in military fashion in companies. They stopped about a mile and a half away. As they did not attack he ordered the officer in charge to challenge the mob and they rode towards a small group, which instantly dispersed. Walton and Rycroft got over a gate and ran away, but he sent a soldier after them who brought them back. When questioned, Lister said that the gate adjoined a road where there were many people who were moving away from the mill.

The next witness, Joseph Briscoll, a sergeant in the Dragoon Guards, said that the cavalry rode up to a small group at a sharp canter. He brought the two men back, but Rycroft was not carrying anything. Overall he had seen thousands of people who were assembled in large gangs.

Sergeant Briscoll arrests Hartley Rycroft

Mr D F Jones then spoke for the prisoner. His long and eloquent defence essentially rested on his assertion that Rycroft was an innocent bystander and he asked the jury to be satisfied regarding the circumstances leading to his arrest for attempting to destroy a mill.

"Now what was the evidence in this case? Did it prove any such thing? He thought not. The Magistrate had admitted that many of the persons assembled were there from curiosity; and he thought the Jury would, from the evidence in this case, be irresistibly led to the

conclusion that Rycroft had gone there from the same motive. They had not seized upon any active and determined ringleader, but upon a poor frightened creature, who, the moment he saw the dragoons cantering up, got out of the road to avoid them. This was his crime – his horrible and inexpiable crime, that he was afraid to remain in the road while a party of dragoons were cantering up to it. Really, if this was an offence, he (Mr Jones) should, in a similar case, be found to be a very wicked offender, for certainly, if he saw a party of dragoons galloping up the road towards him, he should make the utmost possible haste to get out of their way. And then as to the motive which had taken Rycroft there, surely it could not be one of those 'intentions' with which the long indictment against him was full, and which he could not understand if he were to read that indictment from this moment to Christmas time. It could not be any intention to destroy the mill of Messrs Horsfall for he not only was above a mile and a half from that mill, but he had no weapons with him, nor was he doing anything when he was taken by the soldier. Then, what was his motive? The answer was evident. It was curiosity. There could be no doubt that the people in that part of the country had never seen so handsome and well-equipped a set of fellows as those gallant dragoons that the worthy Magistrate had assembled, and the Jury knew well enough, that when such a body of men was turned out, every body went to stare and admire them. This was the case *with Rycroft, and if he was on that account to be treated as an offender against the laws, there was much reason to believe that half the inhabitants of the county would be in the same peril. He put it to the Jury whether, even as a matter of gallantry, they were prepared to say that going to look at the Red-coats was a misdemeanour, for if they were, undoubtedly they must be prepared to convict and punish the great majority of the female race, who were notoriously fond of committing that heinous crime. Surely when the Jury considered all those circumstances, and, the fact, that Rycroft had nothing, and did nothing, they could not avoid acquitting him."*

Rycroft was acquitted.

Tuesday, July 11th
YORK

The three men arrested during and after the riot on the 3rd of May at John Garnett Horsfall's mill at North Wing in Bradford, were John Holdsworth of Clayton, William Bolton of Bradford and James Crowley. The case against Holdsworth and Bolton was made out by Mr Hardy, who explained that the verdict could result in the death penalty. He felt that it was lamentable that in view of the decent appearance of the prisoners they had been led into this offence, which would be proved against them. He added that it was lamentable also that the prisoners believed that destroying machinery would help them. The greatness and prosperity of England depended upon her manufactures, and those manufactures upon the machinery by which they were produced, which, if once destroyed, would, by driving it to other countries lead to ruin. The lawyer argued that men who joined a mob put their lives in danger without thinking that the result could be misery or death. He then went through the events of the day including Holdsworth's alleged role in breaking stones for others to throw at the mill. He had also appeared to be a leader by encouraging the attack and shouting that they would soon be in the mill. In addition he was the person who had spoken to Colonel Tempest and asked him if he expected them to starve.

The first witness, John Ingham, a Bradford constable, said he was in the mill and closed the gates when he saw the mob approaching. When the volleys of stones became intense and an iron stanchion had been wrenched out of a window, the soldiers inside decided that they would have to fire at the crowd for their own safety as a man was trying to climb inside. Ingham had seen one of the prisoners in the lane and one in a field near the mill.

The next witness, Joseph Teesdale, worked at the mill and was in the engine house adjoining when the mob approached. The mill gates had been locked and he couldn't get in so he went to a nearby house. From there he saw John Holdsworth, whom he had known for three years, breaking stones for the two or three hundred attackers to throw at the mill. He didn't see the prisoner throw stones, though he did see him speak to Colonel Tempest.

James Gledhill also saw Holdsworth supplying the rioters with stones and speak to the Colonel about the hard times. He had been stationed in a room in the mill where the windows had been taken out so that he could throw stones down on the mob.

Samuel Ingham was also in the mill on the side where the windows had been taken out and said that he had seen William Bolton outside the mill and throw one stone.

An exchange between Ingham and Bolton throws an interesting light on the relationship between the rioters and the workmen in the mill. The way that language has changed over the years also comes out.

Bolton – *Didst thou see me there Sam?*
Ingham – *I did.*
Bolton – *No thou didn't nor did thou see me throw any stones.*
Ingham – *I did though.*
Bolton – *Sam, didn't thou know me before that day?*
Ingham – *No, I did not.*
Bolton – *Yes thou did, does thou not know that thee and thy brother and me were lads and played together?*
Ingham – *No, I don't.*

A special constable named Gamble said he had seen the rioters march though Bradford. He had also heard Holdsworth, in a harsh manner, ask

Colonel Tempest what they should do about their condition.

The last witness, Timothy Horsfall, explained who the partners were at the mill, that worsted stuffs were manufactured there and that the mill was about half a mile from the town of Bradford. He confirmed that all the windows in the lower storeys were broken and an iron stanchion had been wrenched out from one of them.

Holdsworth and Bolton were allowed to give their accounts of their actions and call witnesses. John Naylor, a weaver from Clayton, said he had passed near the mill and Holdsworth was not taking part in the attack. Sarah Crowther, one of John Horsfall's power-loom weavers said that she had walked to the mill with Holdsworth and he had not taken part in the riot and she did not hear him speak to Colonel Tempest.

The Judge, Sir John Hullock, explained that just assisting a riotous mob was sufficient for the charge to be made. The jury was out for about six hours and found Holdsworth guilty, with a recommendation for mercy and Bolton not guilty. No evidence was put forward against Crowley and he and Bolton were discharged, but bound over for the sum of £50.00. Holdsworth was sentenced to death, the judge observing that some punishment would deter others from committing similar offences. Like the Lancashire rioters tried at Lancaster for similar offences Holdsworth's sentence appears to have been commuted, not to transportation, but to a period of imprisonment.

Wednesday July 12th
York

The trial of Edward Marsh, aged 30, Anthony Miller, aged 19, both of Addingham, and Henry Town, aged 32, of Eastburn began this morning. The charges were similar those of the previous day, having

> " ...unlawfully, riotously, and tumultuously, with other persons, assembled in disturbance of the public peace, and unlawfully and with force begun to demolish a certain mill or building employed in the manufacture of cotton goods, in the occupation of Mr Jeremiah Horsfall."

Timothy Lawson, the manager at Low Mill, said he had prepared for the attack by collecting stones in the mill and taking out some of the windows. When about 150 men came down the mill yard on the north side he asked them what they wanted and they replied that they were going to destroy the power looms. He replied that he pitied their situation and would do what he could to relieve their situation. This they would not accept and said that if there was any resistance they would throw the defenders from the upper windows. The men had axes, hammers and farming implements such as hoes and forks.

The mob then went round to the south side of the mill and after a pistol was fired the attack started. After it had been going on for some time he saw Marsh hold up his hand to a man who was standing by him in the mill and throwing stones down. He shouted, *"I know thee, John Parkinson, and if we don't kill thee to-day we will tomorrow."*

Timothy Lawson told the court that Marsh was a cotton weaver and had a private quarrel with Parkinson, but he had not seen him throwing stones. In all there were twenty-five persons in the mill and about 500 outside, but he admitted that many were probably there out of curiosity.

The former King's Arms in Addingham where Anthony Miller was a stableman.

The second witness, Thomas Carlisle, a dresser (probably a warp dresser for preparing the warp yarns for the power looms) was on the fourth floor in the mill when he saw someone fire a pistol at him. He dodged and in retaliation fired his 'fowling piece' at him, but it exploded and he lost two fingers. There were about twenty men with arms in the mill and he had about ten rounds of ammunition. He had seen Miller go past the mill before the attack started and knew him as an ostler (stableman) at the King's Arms, in Addingham. This public house is now number 25 Church Street, and the stables form a separate building behind.

A third witness. John Shepherd, a workman at the mill, said he had helped to secure the premises and saw the mob approach down the mill yard. He saw Mr Lawson speak to the men and was on a lower floor when the stone throwing started. He then went to the fourth floor and saw Town brandishing a long stake when the people around him were throwing stones. Afterwards he sank down as if wounded. He didn't know if he had been shot, but saw him the next morning being taken along the street on a cart. Town came from Eastburn about four or five miles away. Joseph Harman was in the mill when he was knocked down with a stone. He had seen Town in the mob brandishing a four foot long pole and he had also seen Miller throw stones at the mill. Benjamin Thompson confirmed Mr Lawson's conversation with the rioters and saw Town in the mill yard with the other rioters. He had seen Town bend down to pick up a stone, but didn't see him throw it and knew that he had been shot in the neck.

John Parkinson said he had been in the mill throwing stones down onto the rioters when Marsh, whom he knew, shouted at him that if he was not done for that day he would be the next. The final witness, Richard Lockwood, said that he saw Miller throw stones at the mill building.

Mr Jones, for the defence, submitted that the case for demolishing the mill had not been sufficiently made out. However, Judge Hullock, reflected that the evidence was precisely the same as that in a previous case when the offenders were sentenced to death. Marsh said that he had never injured Mr Horsfall and never intended to do so. Miller and Town said that they were present with the mob, but took no part in the attack and didn't go for that purpose.

Several witnesses gave Marsh a good character reference. One of them, William Cockshott, an Addingham manufacturer, who had employed Marsh as a weaver for seven or eight years, said that he was an honest worthy servant with an excellent character except for a few times when he was drunk.

The judge thought the evidence against the prisoners stronger than in the Bradford case. Breaking the windows did not make their actions a capital felony, but breaking the window frames, which were fixed to the building did. After retiring for about fifteen minutes the jury found all the prisoners guilty, but recommended mercy in consequence of their previous good characters and because, in their opinion, they had been grossly misled. The judge asked on what grounds they made their recommendation and their response was the good character of Marsh and Town and the youth of Miller. All three were sentenced to death for beginning to demolish Mr Horsfall's mill.

In Lancashire the rioters arrested were either sentenced to death or acquitted. The death sentence was always commuted, but some men and women were transported for life with most imprisoned for 18 months or less. The *Leeds Mercury* for Saturday 22nd July carried the following verdicts on the Yorkshire rioters:

> *"The following prisoners were capitally convicted and had judgment of death recorded against them ... Edward Marsh, Anthony Miller and Henry Town, beginning to demolish a mill, at Addingham"*
>
> *"William Bolton and James Crowley, who pleaded guilty to an indictment, charging them with a riot at Bradford, were discharged on their own recognizances"*
>
> *"The following prisoners were acquitted ... Hartley Rycroft and Wm Walton, charged with a riot at Addingham"*
>
> *"... no sentence has been passed against John Holdsworth, convicted of the attack upon Mr. Horsfall's mill, at Bradford"*

There is no record of any of these men being hung, or transported, if the death sentence was transmuted. It is possible that they served a prison sentence.

Tuesday July 18th
Gargrave

Only Joseph Mason from High Mill in Gargrave had machinery destroyed so he applied to the Hundred or Wapentake of Staincliffe for compensation and the case was heard on July 18th. His book-keeper, Paul Bray, described how a mob of between 200 and 300 men armed with guns, swords, hammers and pikes attacked the mill. They broke open the locked door and proceeded to smash the looms. He estimated the damage at £300.

John Holmes, also an employee, was cross-examined by Mr Brougham. He confirmed what had happened, but admitted that Mr Mason had not asked for help from neighbours nor made any resistance, though it was known that other mills had been attacked and the rioters were on their way to Gargrave. The Hundred's lawyers protested that the relevant Act referred only to houses and shops, not factories. The judge decided against this and awarded £300 damages. As a result, for example, Thornton in Craven Parish had to pay £9.14s.9d. as "a proportionate share for power looms damaged belonging to J Mason." This meant, ironically, that some of the rioters who smashed the looms had to pay for the purchase of new looms through the higher poor rates levied on their cottages. The owners of the Addingham and Bradford mills received no compensation for their broken windows and other damage.

Burley-in-Wharfedale

What of school-boy Henry Whitaker whose father dashed away when Greenholme Mill appeared to be threatened? Well, the Harewood and Otley troops of the Yorkshire Hussars were billeted at different places. The officers, under the command of the Hon. Henry Lascelles (later Lord Harewood) were billeted at Greenholme, the millowner's house, which they found very comfortable. They remained there for about six weeks with guards posted on strategic roads at day and night. The gate to Iron Row was locked. The men and horses used some buildings at the end of the old mill as barracks and stables. When the Hussars left Greenholme Mill, Captain Lascelles gave John Whitaker, Henry's elder brother, a dagger he had picked up after the battle of Waterloo.

Monday 24th July
Bradford

The vicar chaired a meeting of the committee for the relief of the poor. William Rand, one of the secretaries, explained that as the payments continued to increase, they could not provide provisions for the coming week. A decision on how to replenish their funds or to continue or discontinue the relief was postponed. However, it was resolved, on the suggestion of Matthew Thompson (a worsted spinner and manufacturer from Westbrook Mill) that the town's surveyors should be asked to call a meeting to consider providing employment for poor people in mending the roads.

The vicar had received £250 for the relief of the poor in Shipley, Clayton and Wilsden by helping to pay wages. In Shipley the work provided for the employed was to be the enclosing of the churchyard.

We have much pleasure in stating, that £250 have been received by the vicar of Bradford, for the relief of the poor in Shipley, Clayton, and Wilsden. This relief is to be given in paying wages for employment; and with respect to Shipley, the employment is, we understand, to be, in inclosing the church-yard. The ceremony of consecration we understand will take place in about six weeks.

Leeds Mercury, 29th July 1826

August 1826
London

The London Committee was still raising money and distributing grants to help relieve the poverty in various parts of the country. Grants to Yorkshire were:

Bradford, additional grant	£700
Heptonstall, additional grant	£150
Midgley, additional grant	£100
Huddersfield, additional grant	£1,000
Southowram	£100
Otley, additional grant	£200
Skipton, for Craven district, additional grant	£1,000

The grant for Bradford was sent to Henry Heap, the vicar. In the letter sent with the grant the London Committee gave advice on how the money should be spent. They were:

"strongly of opinion, that employing the grant to extend the manufacture of goods, would tend to add to the evil, by enlarging the already too great stocks, and by further reducing the price of wages," and *"it would be desirable to employ the poor in mending roads, draining, cutting peat, in short in any way that may lessen the demand upon the fund of the committee."*

However, the committee did express its satisfaction as to how the money was being spent. The Vestry meeting in Bradford had already made provision for work on the roads be made available for those willing, but unable, to work. In addition a suggestion was made to clear out Bradford Beck and it was agreed that a committee of gentlemen be formed to explore that possibility. The Keighley Committee for the relief of the unemployed poor had received £140 from a committee in Skipton.

Colne

The plight of the hand-loom weavers around Colne which led to the thirteen-mile march to attack Low Mill in Addingham on two days in April had worsened by August. The *Leeds Mercury* on the 5th of August carried a feature on the situation there. Reference was made to an appeal for help signed by magistrates, clergymen, churchwardens and overseers sent to Robert Peel in May. This appeal was acknowledged and it was assumed that he had passed the request for help to the London Committee as money had been sent. However, the situation was now far worse. Out of a population of between 7,000 and 8,000 most had been calico weavers, but their jobs were now being taken by power looms. Nine pence a piece was now being paid when previously it had been two shillings and three pence, and eight shillings in 1814. Only a third or a quarter of the people were in employment and five thousand were applying for parish relief. From £60 to £100 a week of free oatmeal was being distributed, paid for by subscription funds from London, Liverpool, Newcastle and local gentlemen. Poor rates had risen to 24 or 25 shillings in the pound, but even with those rates only one shilling each was allowed per week for each person. The writer concluded that:

"Such distress has no parallel in the history of this district. The great and unsaleable stocks of the manufacturers are depreciated from 60 to 100 per cent; the farmers, whose families are chiefly employed in weaving, are on the point of becoming paupers themselves – the poor have not a sufficiency of food – all trade is nearly at a stand, and poor rates equal to the exigencies of the case cannot be collected. Without considerable relief from some quarter, or a speedy and great improvement in trade, certain ruin must soon be the fate of this district."

1827 and later years

So what were the outcomes of the riots in Lancashire and Yorkshire? In the short term the weavers' conditions probably got worse, but the owners of mills where machinery had been smashed were able to seek compensation from the local authority, the Hundred. The Sheriffs' Courts went out of their way to help them with sums being granted for damage as well as the replacement of looms. Mill owners benefited, as the new looms they bought were more efficient, at a time when improvements to looms were rapidly being introduced. The Hundred then recovered the payouts from the poor rate levied on the occupiers of every cottage, house and property. The poor had to pay their share unless they happened to be on poor relief, so many of the rioters had to pay indirectly for the damage they had caused.

The plight of the hand-loom weavers in East Lancashire and West Yorkshire did not improve in the following decades. This unskilled occupation remained at the mercy of trade depressions, each of which reduced the workforce, particularly in the larger towns where other jobs became increasingly available. Slumps in the 1830s and early 1840s brought the most rapid declines. However, hand-loom weaving survived as an activity, if not a full-time occupation, for another thirty years or so. Towards the end of the century it was something the elderly or partially infirm, as well as women, could turn to for a small income. Seasonal workers or others supplemented their wages by weaving a piece of cloth when times were bad. In 1838 there were still nearly 10,000 hand-loom weavers in the parish of Bradford though their income was low as they struggled to compete with the looms in the steam-powered mills. By 1841 the number of worsted power looms at work in Yorkshire was only just over 11,000, but by 1850 it was over 30,000. New types of cloth with a complicated weave saved the hand-loom weavers a niche in which to work, but the growing sophistication of the power looms meant that the advantage rarely lasted.

In the 1830s and 1840s the condition of the poor, such as the new factory workers and specifically of hand-loom weavers was the subject of dozens of Parliamentary enquiries and reports. Select Committees, Poor Law Commissioners and Factory Commissioners all reported on the great changes that were taking place as textile production expanded. This expansion was factory-based, bringing employment for women and children, unsatisfactory urban growth and mounting social problems. Factory production based on the new machines also brought vast wealth to West Yorkshire.

Hand combing also continued as a vital if ill-paid occupation until the 1850s when its demise was sudden with the introduction of the Lister Comb, among others. Attempts to develop successful combing machines had started in the 1790s and continued until the 1850s when most of the difficulties had been overcome. Samuel Cunliffe Lister, a son of E C Lister, used

Low Mill in Addingham for his experimental work and the introduction of his machine comb meant that the last of the hand processes used to produce worsted cloth was no longer needed.

The first power looms, in this account, were introduced into spinning mills by manufacturers who were simply replacing out-workers with machines. They had power supplies, experienced mechanics and mill buildings, so were just modernising their weaving operations and not starting a new venture. The redundant handloom weavers in the Airedale and Wharfedale villages eventually found new jobs in the growing towns of Keighley, Skipton and Bradford. Larger mills in some of the villages also continued to expand, for example Greenholme Mill at Burley-in-Wharfedale, Low Mill at Addingham and Airebank Mill at Gargrave. Weaving sheds were added, particularly when steam power became reliable and cheap, with coal brought in by the new railways. The first weaving shed to be built in Yorkshire was Threaps Shed, or Waterside Mill, at Langcliffe near Settle, which had 800 looms in 1829 for weaving cotton. This, however, was partially water-powered making use of the water from Langcliffe Mill.

It is difficult to reach any firm conclusions about the reasons for the hand-loom weavers in other parts of Yorkshire not rioting. One was probably the growing displacement of the early cotton industry with worsted. It was easy to adapt the early cotton mills built before 1800 to spin worsted. However, the adaptation of cotton machinery to weave worsted yarn was not simple and there were no worsted power looms in or around Halifax, Huddersfield or Keighley in 1826. Therefore the local hand-loom weavers felt secure in their jobs. Power looms were not installed in Keighley worsted mills until eight years after the riots. Keighley was one of the most highly developed textile towns with a growing number of textile machinery manufacturers, but the first looms were brought in only slowly. Perhaps this was an indication of fear of local opposition to power-loom weaving. In addition some of the Bradford merchants who bought worsted cloth were, for a while, against buying pieces woven on power looms.

The growing dominance of worsted over cotton in the West Riding towns began about 1800 and, though never complete, was substantial by 1826. For example, of the thirty cotton-spinning mills in Keighley built before 1800, most were spinning worsted by 1822. In contrast the conversion of Addingham Low Mill to cotton spinning and weaving together with both activities being carried on at Gargrave High Mill was not unexpected in Craven. That area merged into East Lancashire and the opposition to cotton power looms can be understood. Elsewhere, increased supplies of machine-spun worsted yarn just provided more work for the hand-loom weavers in the other Yorkshire towns and villages. Horsfalls at North Wing Mill suffered by being the leaders in using new technology.

A third reason for the containment of the rioting, apart from the presence of the military, was the alternative sources of work being provided in the expanding nearby towns. New mills were steam-powered, with the demand for iron and coal creating new jobs in mining, engineering and transport. It was the hand-loom weavers in their hill top villages who were threatened. They either stuck to the hand loom or gave up their independence for factory work in the town. If those shot during the attack on North Wing Mill provide an indication of the places the other rioters came from, it was the weavers in the hill villages around Bradford who were most fearful for their future, not those in the town itself.

By the 1850s the expansion of the railways, and access to cheap coal, made the building of steam-powered mills in West Yorkshire villages economically viable. Baildon, Wibsey, Eastburn, Cowling and most other villages where the rioters had come from had their own mills, although the jobs were for women, not men. This expansion, though, brought jobs for men with the expanding textile machinery makers and eventually machine tool makers in the towns. It is impossible to say what impact the attacks on the three mills described above had on their owners, or the longer term development of the mills and the firms which ran them. They were at the forefront in installing the latest textile technology and suffered because of that. Nevertheless, others followed and power looms became the norm, though only Low Mill in

Addingham eventually had extensive weaving sheds. All three continued to be used for textile production, but with mixed fortunes which reflected the advantages or otherwise of their situations, the prosperity of their owners and market conditions. North Wing Mill in Bradford became one of hundreds of worsted mills in the city with nothing to distinguish it, apart from its unusual name. The Horsfalls continued at the mill until the 1850s.

High Mill at Gargrave was occupied by Thomas Johnson in 1857 when he was listed as a cotton spinner and manufacturer. Spinning probably stopped in the 1860s and later brakes for trams were made there, but in the early twentieth century it was home to the Ventilated Collar Band Company. The owner of this company, John Gaunt, also built aeroplanes and at the controls of his "Baby" biplane he became one of the first Englishmen to fly at Southport in June 1911. The mill survives as flats, and remains as an example of an early "Arkwright" type mill, many of which were built for cotton spinning throughout the Yorkshire Dales.

Low Mill at Addingham, for a variety of reasons, had an important role in the development of the West Yorkshire textile industries. Jeremiah Horsfall soon added a new mill end on to the existing building and started spinning on mules. Power looms followed without protest, as well as gas lighting. Steam power and other additions followed. However, he was bankrupt in 1841. His brothers John and Timothy Garnett negotiated the lease of the

Low Mill, Addingham around 1950

lease of the mill to William Threlfall, a cotton spinner from Addingham. When he was rendered bankrupt in 1850 the mill reverted to the owners, the Cunliffe-Lister family. Samuel Cunliffe Lister developed his combing machine there, from which he made his first fortune then adapted his machine for combing silk waste. Manningham Mills in Bradford followed and the Lister textile empire became one of the largest in the country. The closure and demolition of all but one of the industrial buildings at Low Mill in 1976 led to the site eventually being developed for housing. However, to the dismay of the owners of the expensive new and refurbished properties, wool scouring was reintroduced between 1999 and 2004. The last remaining mill building, constructed in 1926, has now had an extra floor added and converted to flats. Today, a walk down Low Mill Lane, and between some of the original cottages, will take you on the route taken by the rioters on the 26th April 1826.

Select Bibliography

Public Record Office
HO Correspondence, Disturbances 1812-1855;
HO40/41

Newspapers
Bradford & Huddersfield Courier
Craven Herald
Lancaster Gazette
Leeds Mercury
London Gazette
Morning Chronicle
York Herald

Trade Directories
Baines 1822, Pigot, 1828-9.

Secondary Sources
Aspin, C., *Lancashire.The First Industrial Society*
   (Helmshore, 1969)
Aspin, C., *The Water Spinners* (Helmshore,
   2003)
Baines, Edward, *History of the Cotton
   Manufacture*, London 1835
Balgarnie, R., *Sir Titus Salt*, 1877
Barlow, L. and Smith, R, J.,*The Uniforms of the
   British Yeomanry Force 1794 1914. 3: The
   Yorkshire Hussars*
Bythell, D., *The Handloom Weavers* (1969)
Cudworth, W., *History of Manningham, Heaton
   and Allerton* (Bradford, 1896)
Hodgson, J., *Textile Manufacture in Keighley*
   (Keighley, 1879). Facsimile reprint with an

introduction and index by Gillian Cookson
and George Ingle (Stamford, 1999)

Ingle, G., *Yorkshire Cotton* (Preston, 1997)

James, J., *History of the Worsted Manufacture
in England* (London, 1857)

Jenkins, D.T. & Ponting, K.G., *The British Wool
Textile Industry 1770-1914* (Aldershot, 1987)

Mason, K.M., *Woolcombers, Worsteds and
Watermills*, (Addingham,1989)

Mason, K.M., *Addingham* (Addingham, 1996)

Smith, H. S., *An Alphabetical List of the Officers
of the Yorkshire Hussars* (1853)

Speight, H., *Upper Wharfedale* (Leeds, 1900)

Turner, W., *Riot* (Preston, 1992)

Vavasour, W., Squire of Weston, Diaries, 1797 –
1833

Walker, G., *The Costume of Yorkshire* (London,
1814)

Journals

Scruton, W., 'The Great Strike of 1825', *The
Bradford Antiquary*, Vol.1, Part II,
September 1882

Scruton, W., 'The History of a Bradford Riot',
The Bradford Antiquary, Vol.1, Part III,
September 1884

Ingram Content Group UK Ltd.
Milton Keynes UK
UKHW040637040523
421215UK00001B/37

9 781907 197116